A COMPLETE GCSE COMPUTER STUDIES

Teacher's Guide

Also available from Stanley Thornes (Publishers) Ltd:

Martin Amor & John Fairhurst A COMPLETE GCSE COMPUTER STUDIES Students' Text

Mark Bindley BBC BASIC PROGRAMMING FOR SCHOOLS AND COLLEGES

J. Higgo *et al.* 132 SHORT PROGRAMS FOR THE MATHEMATICS CLASSROOM (Published in co-operation with the Mathematical Association)

A COMPLETE GCSE COMPUTER STUDIES

Teacher's Guide

Martin Amor BA
John Fairhurst BSc

Stanley Thornes (Publishers) Ltd

First published in 1987 by:
Stanley Thornes (Publishers) Ltd
Old Station Drive
Leckhampton
CHELTENHAM GL53 0DN
England

British Library Cataloguing in Publication Data

Amor, Martin
A complete GCSE computer studies—teacher's guide.
1. Electronic data processing
I. Title II. Fairhurst, J. S.
004 QA76

ISBN 0-85950-548-0

Typeset by Blackpool Typesetting Services Ltd, Blackpool
Printed and bound in Great Britain at The Bath Press, Avon

Contents

How We Suggest You Use the Book

DISCUSSION POINTS [?]

We have heavily interspersed the text with questions that we have marked prominently with [?]. These *discussion points* are intended to maximise the teacher's opportunity for involving the class in the theory lessons.

It is the authors' experience that attempts to teach young people about computing by lesson-long lectures are unlikely to be successful.

Such an approach not only fails to kindle enthusiasm for the subject, it also spoonfeeds the class, neglecting one of the most important reasons for studying the applications of computers. Most of the people in the computer industry—from the 'egg-heads' actually designing machines to the analysts working out the requirements for a particular system, and the programmers churning out code—share a common purpose:

> they are designing tools for someone else to use.

The ability to put yourself in someone else's shoes and understand exactly what *they* want the computer to do for *them* is crucial.

Spoonfeeding pupils also fails to train them to look out to see what is happening around them. Good teaching of computer studies must not only acknowledge the ever hastening pace of change but also encourage young people to observe and take an interest in it for themselves. You will know that you have succeeded when *they* bring magazine cuttings to class to show *you* the very latest applications.

With classes of suitable age and character, and in a room with sufficient wall space, you might well organise an information technology (IT) noticeboard and invite students to pin up any relevant articles they may find in the magazines or newspapers they read. That would help keep everybody (including yourself) up to date. A list of suitable sources is included on pages 136–41 of this Teacher's Guide.

OUR APPROACH

We recommend that pupils should read the chapter relevant to a particular topic before you discuss it with them. They should *not* try to do the exercises at the end (which consist of examination style questions) until you have talked about the chapter in class and ensured that the ideas and terminology have been fully understood.

However, they should try to answer all the questions marked **?** when they first encounter them (i.e. before discussing them with you). You might achieve this with some classes by requiring them to read ahead and prepare their answers before a lesson; with others you might organise them into small groups to prepare their answers at the start of the lesson.

JARGON

By 'jargon' we mean the specialist terminology used in computing. But jargon can be deployed as a barrier, as well as an aid, to clear communication. Note that the *Shorter Oxford English Dictionary* warns that the word may be 'applied contemptuously to the cant of a class, sect, trade or profession'.

The jargon listed at the end of each chapter usually follows the order in which the words were introduced in the text (in italics) but has been rearranged occasionally so that appropriate words are grouped together. It is suggested that pupils should write their own notes on each chapter, based on the list of special words, as a summary and revision aid and as a sort of 'vocab book' of computer language.

Although most computing texts provide a glossary, we have deliberately *not* included one. A glossary would short-circuit the 'build-up your own vocab book, chapter by chapter' approach; further, it would encourage students to learn pat phrases of someone else's construction, and in alphabetical order rather than in their proper context. However, we *have* provided an extensive index so that students can find out the meaning and setting of any word or phrase they require. We have taken as a guide to spellings and style the British Computer Society's 'Glossary of computing terms' (5th Edition, 1987; ISBN 0 521 33261-3; Cambridge University Press).

TEACHING ORDER

We have laid out the material in what seems to us to be a logical order, and we have deliberately *not* followed some of the more traditional patterns.

We have set out to develop the idea of the computer as a tool before attempting to deal with the headier mathematics and logic theory (Inside the CPU, Part E).

Obviously, the precise order of teaching the material depends on your individual preferences, your syllabus, and your class. Part E is largely self-contained and could be covered at any time in the course.

THE TEACHER'S GUIDE

This guide includes plenty of supporting material expanding on the ideas raised as discussion points. We have also made occasional suggestions relevant to the harder examination questions in the exercises that conclude each chapter.

KEEPING UP TO DATE

The Computer Studies teacher faces the problem of keeping abreast of subject matter that changes very rapidly. For this reason, this teacher's guide is in loose-leaf form; not only will you be able to add your own amendments and lesson notes but also, periodically, we shall issue updated pages for insertion into the guide. These will be advertised in Stanley Thornes' annual catalogue.

COPYRIGHT

Part A Overview

1 Introduction

The Introduction shows that computers are already part of normal daily life; they are not used just by space agencies, huge corporations and keen hobbyists. Many applications of computer technology are not immediately obvious, as the story of George and Linda demonstrates.

DISCUSSION POINTS

? **Q 1.1** The section, 'Technology behind the scenes', which follows in the chapter, gives a number of applications; students may well come up with others. For each example of computer use students should try to work out what kinds of information are being handled. Information and data are defined more strictly later in this chapter, but do not worry about the distinction for now.

For example, the washing machine processor needs to 'know' whether it is dealing with delicate items, what the water temperature should be, how long to spin, how many times the load has been spun, and so on. The cash dispenser, on the other hand, must 'know' whether the number keyed in is valid, the drawing limit for that particular person, how much she has already withdrawn that week, and what to do if three incorrect numbers are keyed in in succession (usually swallow the card).

? **Q 1.2** The obvious ones will be any home or school microcomputers. Modern hi-fi systems, televisions, video recorders, washing machines and many other appliances use microprocessors. Telephones with dials usually do not have silicon chips, but those with push-buttons and memories do. How many students are wearing quartz watches, *including* those with a conventional face and hands? They all have chips. If there is a clock in the classroom, ask students whether it uses a microchip or not. But be careful. The chances are that it does not; it is probably driven by an ordinary electric motor. By contrast, most *smaller* electric clocks today, especially battery-driven ones, *do* have microchips in their movements.

? **Q 1.3** Some examples:

1. the time for which the alarm clock was set (which the microprocessor compares with the actual time *every minute*)
2. the temperature of the shower water
3. the fabric setting of the washing machine
4. the temperature setting on the iron
5. the exact location of the cutting blade on the automatic pattern-cutter which cut George's suit (measured, say, by the distances from the front and from the left-hand edge of the cutting table)
6. the atmospheric pressure and temperature used in the weather forecast
7. the weight of bran flakes automatically put into the packet
8. the amount owing as printed on George and Linda's bill
9. the speed (say 2 m.p.h.) at which George was crawling in the traffic jam
10. the office telephone number stored in George's car telephone
11. the number of the track which the compact disc player was playing
12. the digital codes representing the music itself
13. the speed limit relayed for display on the overhead signs
14. the pressure exerted by George on the brake pedal
15. the speed of rotation of George's road wheels
16. the amount of cash drawn out by Linda (and her bank balance etc.)
17. the details of the job vacancy to operate a Honshu 2000 word processor (this is an imaginary make)
18. the date recorded on the library computer when Linda's books were due back, and the book details
19. the amounts 'rung up' at the supermarket checkout
20. Linda's chargecard code, her credit limit and her outstanding balance
21. George's rate of consuming fuel.

This is not, of course, an exhaustive list; there are thousands of items of data involved.

? **Q 1.4** Take some of the above examples of data. The alarm clock processor compares the two items of data (actual time and alarm time), and does nothing except carry on displaying the actual time until the two times match exactly. Then it either sounds the alarm or starts the radio (depending on how George and Linda have set, or *programmed*, it).

The temperature of the shower water is also compared with fixed data, i.e. the desired temperature which George *dialled* on the control knob. The action taken if the temperatures do not match depends on the type of shower. If the shower heats cold water, the heating element is turned up/down (or on/off). If it works by mixing preheated water with cold water, then the mix is altered by adjusting valves.

The location of the fabric cutting blade would be input many times per second to the controlling computer, until a required position was reached. Then the blade might be instructed to stop, or change direction, all under program control.

The amount owing, printed on the bill, was the result of a previous calculation: units consumed times price per unit (two of the input data items). The amount would not only be printed on the bill; it would be simultaneously stored on a computer file containing many accounts, including George and Linda's. Later, when they send a cheque or transfer cash to pay the bill, the amount paid is input to the system and compared with the amount owing. If there is still a balance owing, a reminder letter is sent.

The speed of George's car is input to the *trip computer* along with the rate of fuel consumption, calculated by:

$$\frac{\text{speed in m.p.h.}}{\text{fuel used in g.p.h.}}$$

George was shocked at his terrible fuel consumption, which might have been as low as 6 m.p.g., but this is not too surprising for crawling along in a traffic jam.

? **Q 1.5** Most washing machines are reprogrammable to a limited extent (even if only to vary, say, the water temperature or length of spin) and some are quite sophisticated. But they are obviously not programmable in the wider sense; a washing machine could not add two numbers together. A hi-fi system may be reprogrammable (if you can preselect tracks, change the sequence or set it to repeat a record) and a digital alarm clock is reprogrammable (you can set the time, set the alarm or change from buzzer to radio) but both are extremely limited in the range of possible programs. The home computer is infinitely reprogrammable (or at least until it wears out).

? **Q 1.6** This question may look trivial, but it is well worth getting everyone to do it. It is one thing to read in a textbook how fast, or how accurate, computers are compared to people, and quite another to understand it. This exercise will give students a practical insight into the phenomenal speed of computers and demonstrate the scale of the problems of human error.

? **Q 1.7** Most of the examples in fact involve calculations too rapid or involving too much data for a human being to handle. Examples of the highest speed are in the anti-lock braking system and in decoding the weather satellite transmissions (which also entails huge volumes of data).

2 Computer Systems

DISCUSSION POINTS

? **Q 2.1** Estimates of the likely cost will vary considerably, depending on the microcomputer and printers chosen. Most students will probably under-estimate the cost. They will also neglect to include the cost of the disk interface and leads, which could amount to a further £100 or more beyond their 'planned' spending. This is not an uncommon error for business users too.

? **Q 2.2** If a computer is linked to an ordinary TV set, through the conventional aerial socket, then signals must pass through the TV's amplification system which causes some loss of quality. The poor quality image can be a strain to work with for long periods (e.g. on a word processing job) and can detract from the graphics effects of games or educational software.

A proper monitor conveys the computer's signals directly to the screen with no loss of quality. The electron beams that form the image are also more accurately controlled. Monitors tend to cost more than TV sets because of the relatively small volume of sales. Some TV sets now include a monitor option.

? **Q 2.3** A colour monitor costs significantly more than a black and white one (at least twice and probably three times as much). A home computer system would need colour, for computer games and educational programs depend a great deal upon impressive graphics and would fall rather flat in black and white. Colour was, until recently, regarded as an expensive luxury for business users; colour is not essential for successful word processing, spreadsheet and accounts programs. However, increasing use of graphics packages and more complex displays is leading companies to use colour.

On the other hand, a business would need disk drives for rapid storage and retrieval of data; and preferably *dual* disk drives (probably including one hard disk) to ensure that staff make back-up copies of all their disk-based records. A business would also need a letter-quality printer for its word processing system. Home systems could easily do without either.

? **Q 2.4** The problems include:
(i) security: access to some information may need to be restricted
(ii) protection of information: someone may incorrectly alter centrally held information

(iii) breakdown of system: entire operation could fail
(iv) communications links might be troublesome.

? **Q 2.5** The ageing telephone network is not the most reliable medium for the transmission of data; also it works with analog signals, i.e. continuously varying rather than on/off signals. Data transmitted this way must therefore be sent and received through special equipment (*modems*) and incorporate a check digit with every byte transmitted; even so there is still danger that information will be corrupted. The position is steadily improving, however, as British Telecom updates its lines.

There is also the possibility of a member of the public (a so-called hacker) breaking into confidential files if the pass-codes are not elaborate enough.

Most business users transmitting data in this way rent special lines from BT rather than going through the public telephone network.

? **Q 2.7** 07 03 88 could represent the 7th March 1988 to a European but July 3rd to an American. Identical data can represent quite different information according to interpretation. These same six digits could equally be a telephone number, a serial number or other code.

? **Q 2.8** (*a*) Analog devices: thermometer, pressure gauge, barometer, clock or watch with hands, sundial, spring balance

(*b*) Digital devices: digital clock, electronic weighing machines.

? **Q 2.9** Because computers work in the binary (base 2) number system.

? **Q 2.10** No. However, the amount of memory available to the user is not always as much as it seems. The operating software uses up some RAM. For example, the BBC computer has seven screen modes and each mode uses a different number of bytes for the screen display. Thus a user working in mode 3 has very much less memory available than if he or she worked in mode 7.

? **Q 2.11** Some students will need help to work out this sum. Every student should get a different answer, for they will have different handwriting sizes and different line lengths. However, it should be a useful exercise that helps them to realise the significance of '128 K of memory space'.

EXERCISES 2

Q 5 Modern computers are digital not only because of the greater accuracy of digital representation but also because of a number of other advantages, e.g. ease of programming, greater versatility and the ease of mass-producing circuits.

Continuous variables (such as temperature) are digitised (e.g. to '36.6 °C') whenever a reading is taken.

Part B
Communicating with the Computer

3 Writing Good Programs

This chapter should be deferred until students are well under way with the programming side of the course. It assumes that they have already written a good number of short programs and understand elementary BASIC statements such as FOR . . . NEXT and IF . . . THEN. PROCedures figure prominently.

THE PROGRAMS

All the programs (except those written in LOGO or Pascal) are written in BBC BASIC and will run on the BBC or Electron computers.

The only significant departures from standard BASIC are the PROCedure statements which effectively call a subroutine by name (rather than line number) and the use of ' after a PRINT statement to cause the computer to insert a blank line. In standard BASIC the equivalent to

10 PROCinput	is	10 REM Begin input procedure at line 1000 20 GOSUB 1000

and to

10 PRINT "Hi" '	is	10 PRINT "Hi" 20 PRINT

BBC BASIC allows variable names of any length, but will not accept them as two words; they may be hyphenated, however, with the underline symbol. Hence we use variable names such as data_item. This is also likely to be different on other machines.

We have deliberately not suggested answers to the programming problems set, for these will be different from machine to machine and from pupil to pupil. However, we have unscrambled the listings that appear in the main text.

FLOWCHARTS: FURTHER POINTS

Flowcharts are intended to depict algorithms simply, and yet students often produce mammoth charts that are sometimes more complex than the programs themselves.

We suggest you should strongly emphasise the 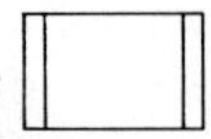 symbol for a subroutine or procedure (and in doing so, promote good programming practice) even though some Boards do not include it in their lists of flowchart symbols.

We also suggest that, as soon as students start to handle problems of sufficient complexity, you relax the 'yes/no exits only' rule for decision boxes. (We have not written this into the text for it offends some traditionalists.) The British Computer Society Schools Committee has recommended the alternative forms shown in Figs. 3.1 (*a*)–(*c*).

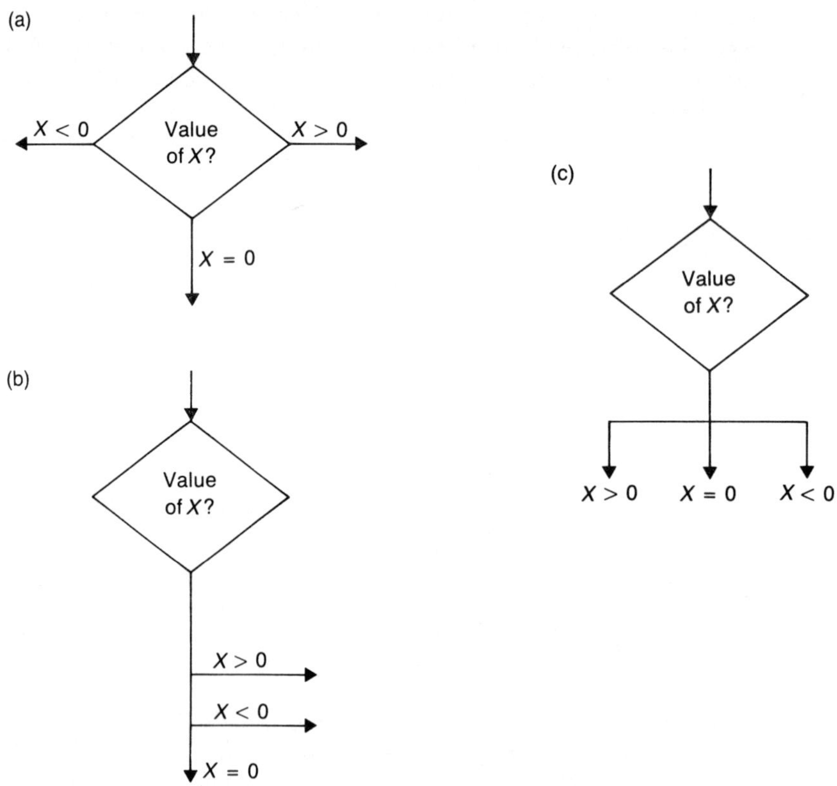

Fig. 3.1 Decision boxes for flowcharts

The styles in (*b*) and (*c*) can be extended to any number of cases [not just the three as in (*a*)]. Of course students should still be made aware that the basic yes/no control structure is sufficient, if repeated often enough, to chart any multi-tiered decision.

DISCUSSION POINTS

Answers to these *top down* problems will vary considerably. Accept any diagram that makes the point. Our suggestions are illustrated below. Note that we have assumed that jobs on the same tier in the diagram must be ordered left to right.

? **Q 3.1**

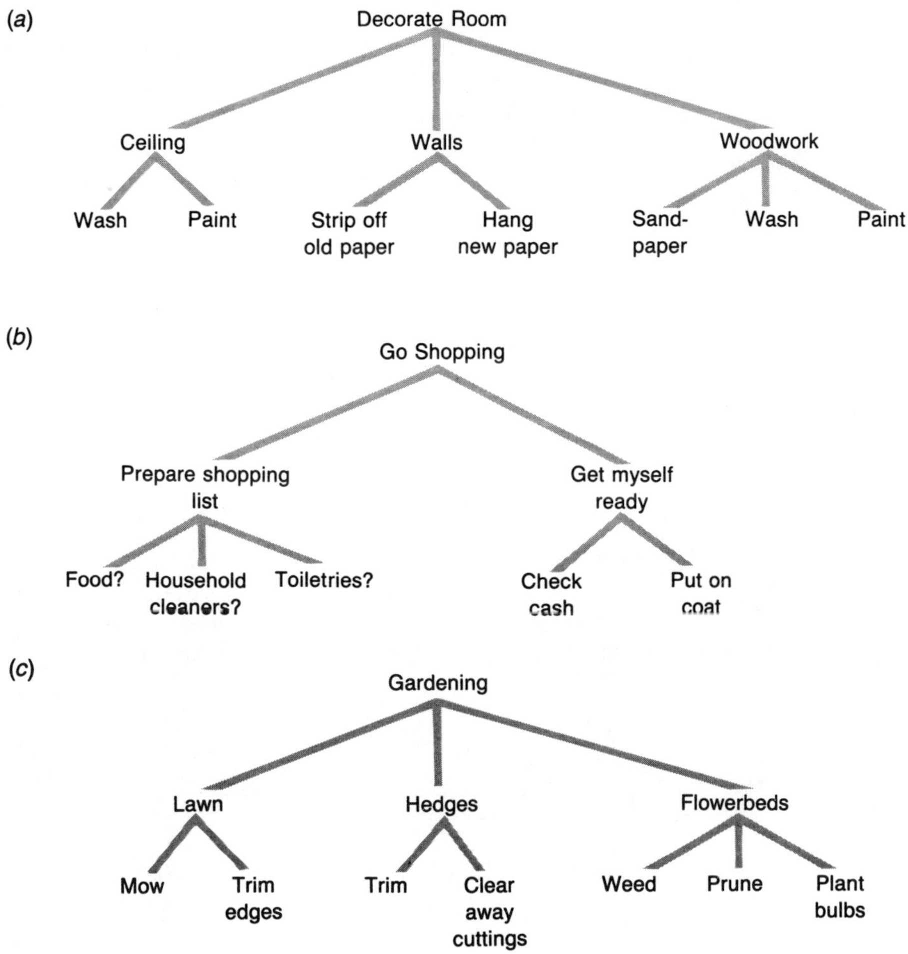

Fig. 3.2

? **Q 3.2**

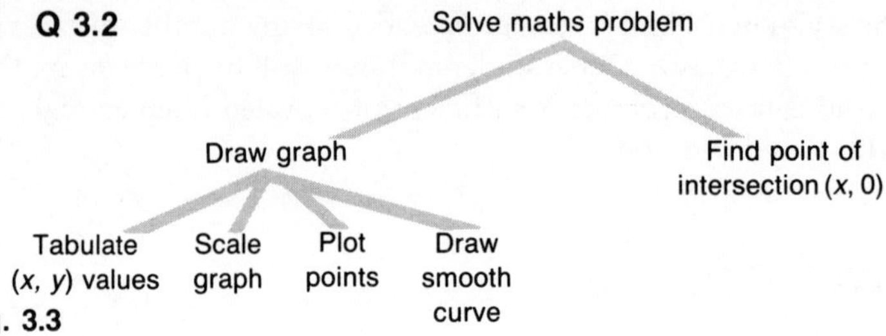

Fig. 3.3

? **Q 3.3**

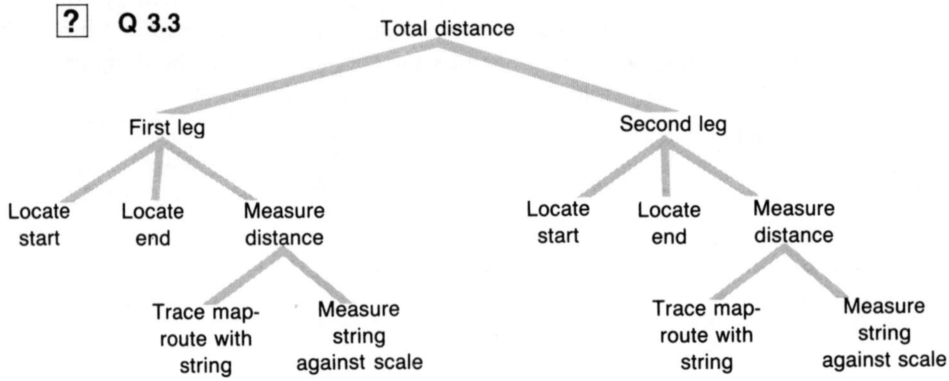

Fig. 3.4

? **Q 3.4**

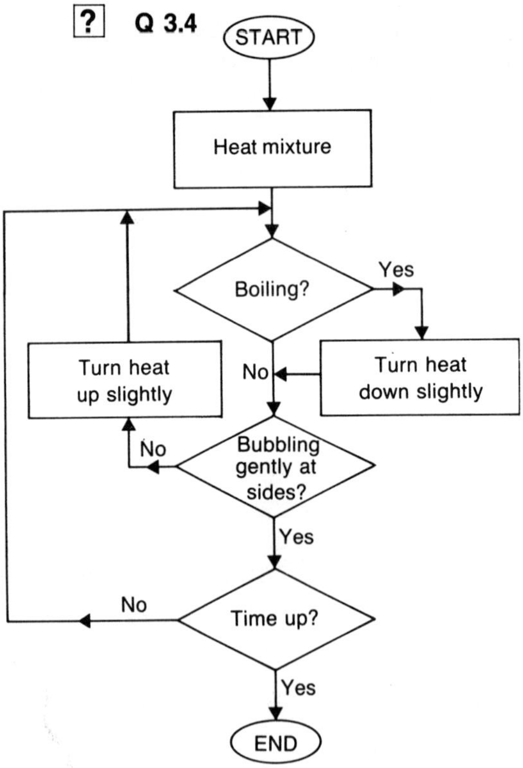

Fig. 3.5 (*a*) Simmer algorithm

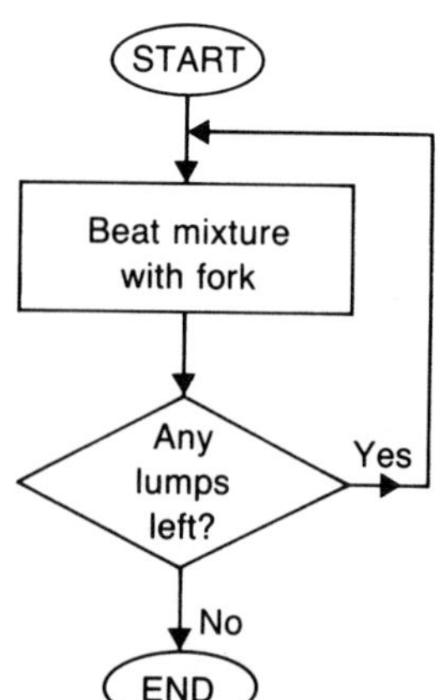

Fig 3.5 (*b*) Mash algorithm

? **Q 3.5**

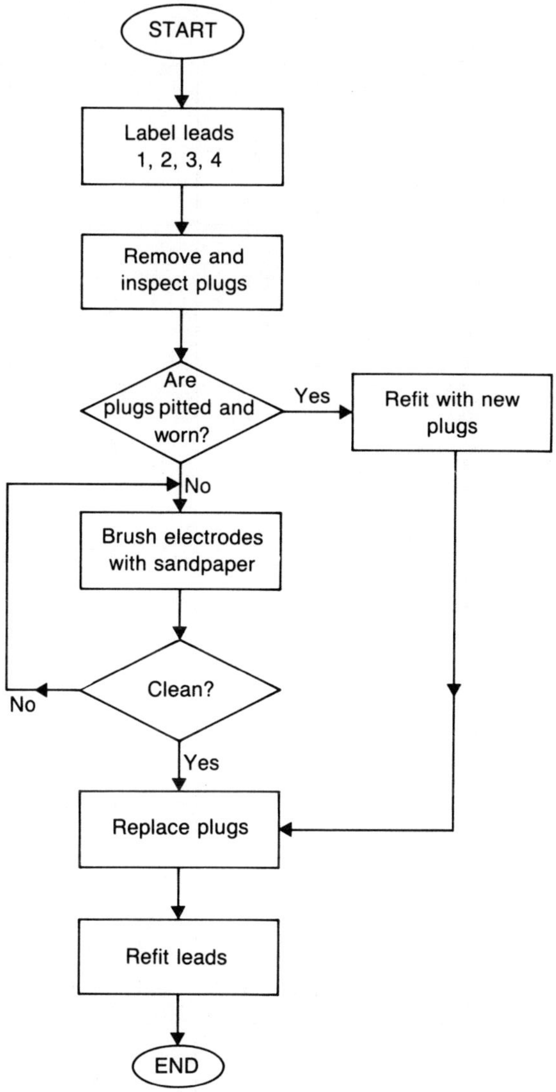

Fig. 3.6 (*a*) Flowchart for servicing spark plugs

? **Q 3.6**

Step	Data	Count	Count < 10?	Total	Output
1		0		0	
2	2				
3				2	
4		1			
5			Yes		
6	3				
7				5	
8		2			
9			Yes		
10	6				
11				11	
12		3			
13			Yes		
14	7				
15				18	
16		4			
17			Yes		
18	5				
19				23	
20		5			
21			Yes		
22	13				
23				36	
24		6			
25			Yes		
26	17				
27				53	
28		7			
29			Yes		
30	18				
31				71	
32		8			
33			Yes		
34	12				
35				83	
36		9			
37			Yes		
38	9				
39				92	
40		10			
41			No		
42					9.2

? Q 3.8

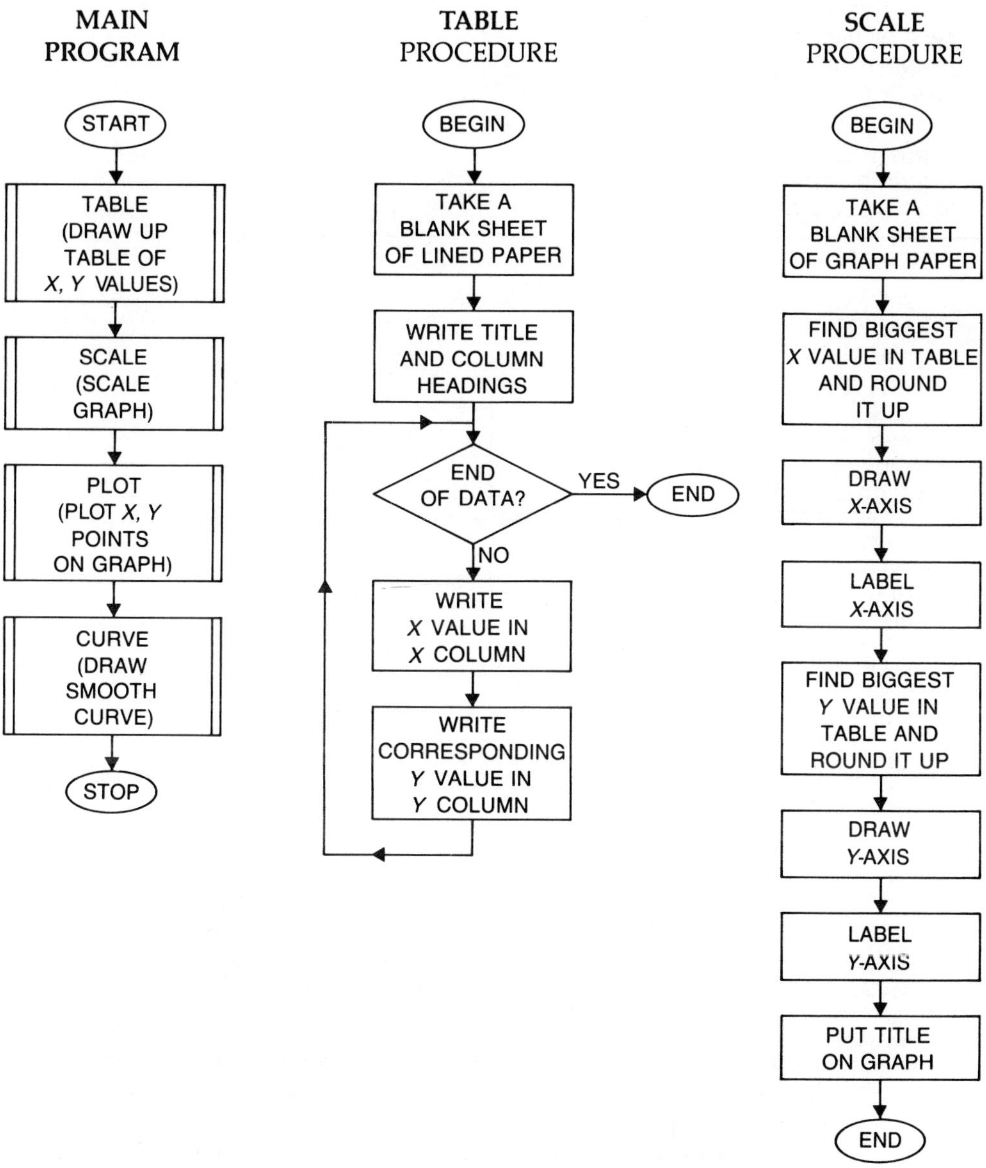

Fig. 3.6 (*b*) Flowchart for drawing a graph

PLOT
PROCEDURE

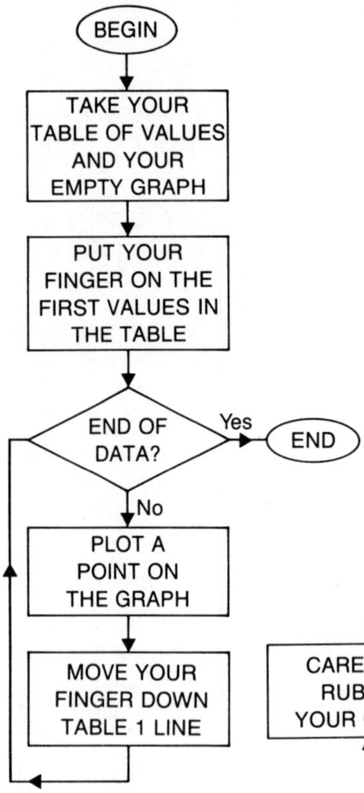

CURVE
PROCEDURE

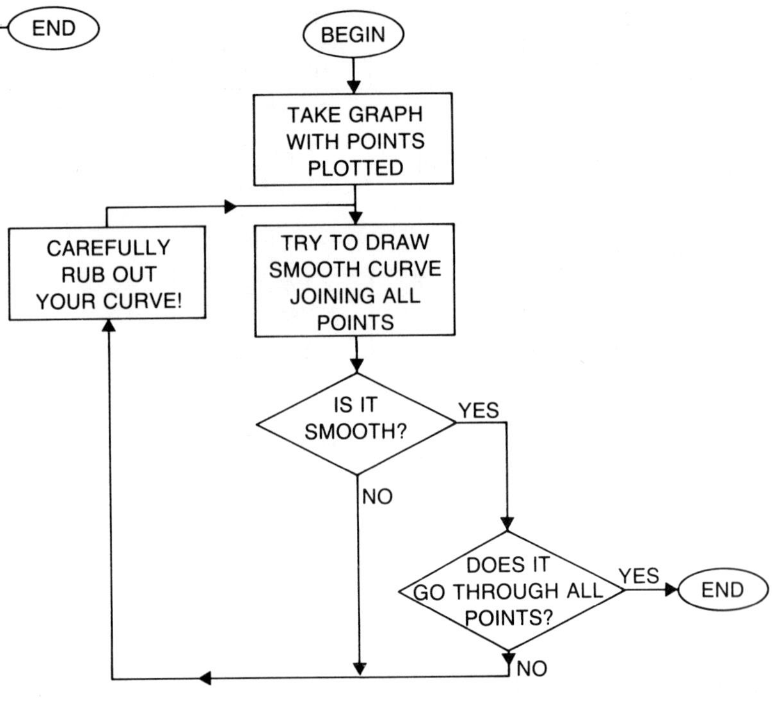

One final point on flowcharts: we are aware that some computing educationalists are currently arguing that students should prepare their algorithms in pseudo-code or other cryptic form; flowcharts are out of fashion! We regret this, fearing that it will encourage pupils to code-as-they-go (especially the weaker ones for whom the distinction between preparing a program in advance in pseudo-code and writing it straight out in BASIC is far too subtle to grasp). The clarity and simplicity of a flowchart and, above all, the obvious difference from program code will, in our view, best help teenagers understand and undertake the procedures of good program writing.

? **Q 3.9**

Step	H	L	X	X = O?	X > H?	X < L?	Output
1	0	999 999					
2			5				
3				No			
4					Yes		
5	5						
6						Yes	
7		5					
8			12				
9				No			
10					Yes		
11	12						
12						No	
13			15				
14				No			
15					Yes		
16	15						
17						No	
18			8				
19				No			
20					No		
21						No	
22			0				
23				Yes			
24							15, 5

Step	H	L	X	X = O?	X > H?	X < L?	Output
1	0	999 999					
2			3				
3				No			
4					Yes		
5	3						
6						Yes	
7		3					
8			2.1				
9				No			
10					No		
11						Yes	
12		2.1					
13			0.3				
14				No			
15					No		
16						Yes	
17		0.3					
18			5				
19				No			
20					Yes		
21	5						
22						No	
23			7.3				
24				No			
25					Yes		
26	7.3						
27						No	
28			0				
29				Yes			
30							7.3, 0.3

The algorithm selects the highest and lowest in a set of numbers between 0 and 999 999. Zero is used as a *terminator* or *rogue value*; it is *not* part of the data but terminates the loop so that the values of H and L (the highest and lowest numbers) are output. It is worth mentioning that had the variables H and L been given meaningful names, e.g. 'highest' and 'lowest', no one in the class would have found difficulty in establishing what was happening as they worked through the algorithm.

? **Q 3.13** Numeric variable B may be *input* as text e.g. "TEN". The BBC microcomputer will accept text and assign the value 0; other machines may well reject the error out of hand. Either way, there needs to be an error trap.

? **Q 3.14** When a program crashes, the ON ERROR function will cause the computer to follow a procedure arranged by the programmer instead of that built in by the manufacturer (which usually stops the run with some unfriendly message such as 'SYNTAX ERROR LINE 110').

? **Q 3.16** Students should be encouraged to look back at one of their own programs, for there is no better way for the point to be made. However, this might not be practical if the students have no record of their earlier programs or have only written very short ones which they can work out again fairly easily. You may prefer to write out one of your own programs, suitably scrambled to make it hard to follow, or find one in a magazine or even in the computer manual.

? **Q 3.17** A = number of data items; B = cumulative total and
C = data item

The program will run and will find the mean of a set of data if the user knows how to respond to the ? prompt when it appears on the screen.

? **Q 3.18** The program 'Mean Averages' has not included any error traps, which are essential for a good program. Thus entering text, or non-positive or noninteger values for number_of_items will cause problems, as will entering text for one of the data_items.

? **Q 3.19** Those books that suggest handwritten annotations of a program listing were presumably written a few years ago when the constraints on memory space were a lot tighter. Clearly, such handwritten comments save a lot of computer memory and will be very prominent if written in colour. However, where there is space available, it is better to annotate the program with REM statements so that the asides are actually part of the program and cannot be lost (unless the program is lost) or separated from it.

? **Q 3.20**

```
10 REM Multiples
20 REM
30 REM = = = = = = = = = = = = = = = = = = = = = = = = = = = = = =
40 REM Variables Used
50 REM ----------------------
60 REM multiplier = first number in sequence (input by user)
70 REM count = loop counter
80 REM
```

```
90 REM ============================
100 REM Initialise variables
110 REM ---------------------------
120 LET multiplier = 0
130 REM
140 REM ============================
150 REM Clear screen, give instructions and input multiplier
160 REM ------------------------------------------------------------------------
170 CLS
180 PRINT "The program lists the first 14 multiples of the
number you type"
190 PRINT ' ' "Type in your number then press RETURN" ' '
200 REPEAT
210 INPUT "Your number is? " multiplier ' '
220 REM
230 REM Error Trap
240 REM ----------------
250 REM Computer assigns value zero to multiplier if user
inputs text
260 REM Zero itself is another nonsensical input and is also
trapped
270 REM
280 IF multiplier = 0 THEN PRINT '' "Eh? " '' "Try again,
please."''
290 REM
300 UNTIL multiplier <> 0
310 REM
320  REM ==========================
330 REM Output routine
340 REM ----------------------
350 FOR count = 1 TO 14
360 PRINT count * multiplier
370 NEXT count
380 PRINT '''
390 END
```

[?] **Q 3.21**

```
10 REM Fibonacci Numbers
20 REM
30 REM ============================
40 REM Variables used
50 REM ----------------------
60 REM A and B both represent alternate numbers in Fibonacci
sequence
70 REM J = loop counter
80 REM
90 REM ============================
100 REM Initialise Variables
110 REM ---------------------------
120 LET A = 1
130 LET B = 1
140 REM
150  REM ==========================
160 REM Output and update loop
170 REM ------------------------------------
```

```
180 REM
190 FOR J = 1 TO 5
200 REM Output current values of A and B
210 PRINT A
220 PRINT B
230 REM -------------------------------
240 REM Update values
250 LET A = A + B
260 LET B = A + B
270 NEXT
280 END
```

? **Q 3.22**

```
10 REM Dice Simulator Program
20 REM
30 REM ============================
40 REM Variables Used
50 REM -----------------------
60 REM score = random score (between 1 and 6) generated
by computer
70 REM count = loop counter
80 REM pause = count in time-wasting loop
90 REM
100 REM ==========================
110 REM Generate score and display result
120 REM --------------------------------------------------
130 REM
140 LET score = RND(6)
150 FOR count = 1 TO score
160   PRINT "#";
170   VDU(7)
180   REM short pause
190      FOR pause = 1 TO 1000
200      NEXT pause
210 NEXT count
220 PRINT ' ' '
230 REM ==========================
240 REM Long pause then start again
250 REM -------------------------------------------
260      FOR pause = 1 TO 4000
270      NEXT pause
280 RUN
```

? **Q 3.23** The problem is not as bad as it looks. The program simply prints **THE GOTO SHOW** (at line 120).

? **Q 3.24** Yes, if the turtle is initially facing right and is placed on the left-hand side of the screen.
Other initial orientations give different results.
For example, if the turtle were facing up the screen initially, the program gives the shape shown.

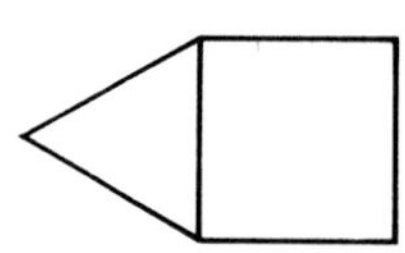

Ask pupils to devise similar, simple LOGO programs 'TO HOUSE' from different initial positions.

Incidentally, LOGO is not simply a children's language. It is essentially a list processing language, derived from LISP, and can be extended way beyond the simple illustrations we have given in the pupils' text.

4 Types of Software

Students (and many other computer users) still tend to overestimate the importance of the machine itself and underestimate the importance of the software needed to use it. They should also be aware of the variety of forms which software takes. It is easy to be completely *unaware*, when loading a program into a microcomputer, that there is some crucially important software in it already.

DISCUSSION POINTS

? **Q 4.1** The main reason is that software requires a lot of people (whose time is expensive) to develop it. Hardware manufacture can be (and has been) substantially automated. Some steps have been taken towards automating software production (with fourth generation languages and program generators) but progress is slow. Computer people, it seems, are happy to help automate other people's work but not their own.

A further reason is the increasing sophistication which computer users are coming to expect of software; they now demand powerful features and reliable programs that are extremely easy to use. They are no longer willing to attend lengthy training courses before they can start using the software. This means a lengthier (and therefore costlier) development cycle.

? **Q 4.2** Applications, but point out that no games program could run without some systems software in ROM to permit loading and running.

? **Q 4.3** Most students should think of disk drives, tape drives (if applicable) and printers (and/or plotters). Fewer will remember the screen (monitor or TV) and the keyboard (often the two most important peripherals). Any other devices in use (e.g. joysticks, light pens, tablets or 'mice') should be included, as they are all peripheral devices.

? **Q 4.4** If your school or college has a powerful microcomputer which several people can use at once, then it is a multiprogramming system. A *network* of microcomputers is different; the computers may share resources (e.g. storage and printers) but each CPU usually runs a single program (unless it has a *concurrent* operating system).

All large companies use multiprogramming computers that can, for example, run the payroll, respond to stock enquiries and test programs under development, all at the same time. Another common use of multiprogramming is in universities, where students and academics can run hundreds of different programs on one machine.

? **Q 4.5** There is very little compatibility between operating systems for the microcomputers that are common in education. The early machines in schools had the following:

BBC 'B' — Acorn's own operating system
RML 380Z — CP/M (widespread on 8-bit micros)
Sinclair Spectrum — Sinclair's own operating system.

Later additions include add-on ROM to enable the BBC to run the CP/M operating system and

RML Nimbus — MS-DOS (industry standard : 16-bit)
BBC Master Series — Acorn's OS 3, but MS-DOS and CP/M-86 on the 512 model.

? **Q 4.6** 1. They may be written in the assembly language for different chips, e.g. Z80A (Spectrum), 6502 (BBC).

2. Games often use other features peculiar to one machine, e.g. 'sprite' graphics, ways of storing screen images, colour ranges, sound etc.

3. If the operating systems are incompatible, games written on other systems will not load.

? **Q 4.7** A string such as 'FRED' has no numeric value and so cannot be added to anything. (Note: Some versions of BASIC, notably BBC, will in fact give 'FRED' a numeric value of 0, but it is bad practice to rely on this; other versions of BASIC would abort the program.)

An INPUT statement must include a variable name, so that the system has somewhere to store the input. 999 is not a variable name.

? **Q 4.8** There is still no accepted industry standard for BASIC: Microsoft BASIC is now very widespread since IBM adopted it.

Acorn (BBC), Research Machines, Commodore and Sinclair have all gone their own ways. Sinclair launched *four* successive, incompatible versions of BASIC with its first four machines (ZX80, ZX81, Spectrum and QL), before Amstrad bought their range.

The problem is, again, one of portability. Programs written in one dialect simply will not run on a machine that uses another. Software companies therefore have to spend many hours rewriting programs. Teachers cannot use software or programming examples unless they have the same machine as the author.

? **Q 4.9** If students have found this difficult, make it into a small project for individual research. See pages 136–41 of this guide for useful sources of information which they can consult.

? **Q 4.10** Built-in ROM:

- Instantly available to the system
- Less danger of corruption
- Does not use up RAM
- Fast access speed

Supplied on disk:

- Easier to change language (e.g. from Pascal to COBOL)
- Easier to load new releases (i.e. enhanced or debugged versions)
- Interpreter can often be larger (and hence more sophisticated).

? **Q 4.11** Certainly; they just happen to be stored on paper. Even an algorithm or flowchart is software; it represents the *potential* instructions to the computer to achieve a desired result.

5 Input

DISCUSSION POINTS

? **Q 5.1** A direct infra-red link is on-line; it is preferable to a cable link as the keyboard is then fully manoeuvrable (at least within a short range of the computer) but there is the possibility of interference from external sources.

? **Q 5.2** There are many examples of off- and on-line uses of a computer. The most obvious might be:

on-line: almost all home computer uses, process control systems, bank cash dispensers, travel agents' booking systems.
off-line: clerical and accounting systems that might be processed as a batch later (library stock information; supermarket chain daily sales data etc.).

? **Q 5.3** The QWERTY keyboard was designed deliberately as an *inefficient* keyboard in order to keep typing speeds down. The world's first production typewriter, a Remington, was not an immediate success because the keys kept jamming, and so to reduce possible typing speeds a new layout was devised. The inefficiencies are obvious; A, E, I and O are all awkwardly placed and the index fingers control such little-used keys as Y, V and J.

Attempts were made at the turn of the century to design an improved layout, but by then QWERTY was a *de facto* standard. Today, we have the same problem, although mechanical considerations are completely irrelevant to our electronic systems.

There is interest in the USA in a new keyboard layout in which all the vowels and the most common consonants (D, H, T, N, S) are controlled by the 'home keys' (where a touch-typist rests the fingers). It is claimed that 70% of all English words can be typed without moving the fingers off the home keys. It remains to be seen whether this keyboard will find general favour. VDE may make keyboards out of date anyway!

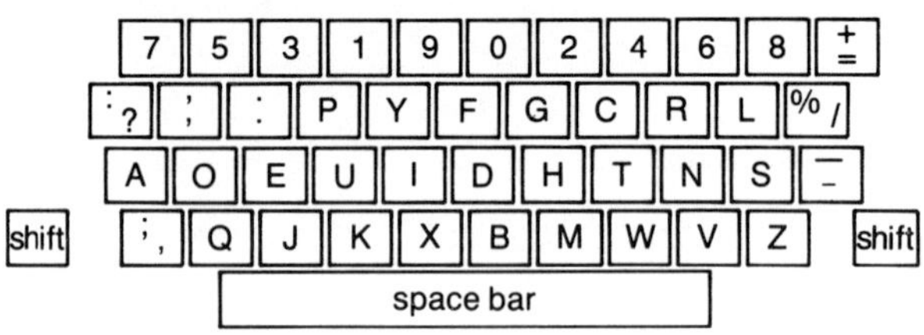

Fig. 5.1 Logical lettering: Dvorak's DSK keyboard

? **Q 5.4** If the same operator keys in the same data, then it is fairly likely that some of the errors will be repeated and therefore *not* put right. A second operator ensures completely independent verification.

? **Q 5.5** Validation. If a keyboard can spot this type of error then it has 'intelligence' of its own, i.e. an on-board microchip preprogrammed to accept numeric input only at that point. (Verification is simply a clerical routine independent of software.)

? **Q 5.6** ROM cartridges are expensive because of the software they carry.

? **Q 5.7** Dongles are protection devices; programs recorded on tapes and disks are easy to copy illegally (as most home-computer hobbyists are well aware). A dongle makes life rather more difficult for the would-be pirate.

Piracy is an important headache to the software industry; copyright laws (although recently amended to include software) are still not really adequate to cope with the problems associated with the new technology, as in other areas, e.g. video.

Certainly, sections of *code* are protected by copyright law (as, for example, sections from this book). But the inventiveness and genius of a software house lies in the *methods* of its solutions, not in line-by-line code. Is it possible to copyright an algorithm? Or the 'look' and 'feel' of a program? The law has yet to be properly tested.

? **Q 5.8** Most data that is put on a computer arrives there through a keyboard. It is *not* likely that other developments will supercede it until reliable VDE systems allow operator and machine to communicate directly.

The mouse and other alternatives to the keyboard are attractive to occasional computer users who do not type (a company executive for example). Their use is mainly restricted to choosing options displayed on screen. Many keyboard operatives (secretaries, journalists etc.) will use the keyboard linked to a computer in order to *ease* the problem of typing, editing and retyping (see Chapter 13 and the example of word processing), *not* to replace it.

? **Q 5.9** As the computer 'learns' its vocabulary from the person who will direct it, then *any* given sound could mean 'go right' however meaningless a grunt it appears to the rest of us. All that matters is that the sounds for 'go right', 'go left', 'stop' etc. are sufficiently different for the computer to tell them apart.

? **Q 5.10** The 13-digit code is usually printed with the first digit to the left of the bar code. An article packaged in Britain (although *not* necessarily made in Britain) begins with '5'. Those that begin '3' are packaged in France; those that begin '4' are packaged in West Germany, and so on.

You can find a French bar code on Gillette shaving cream aerosol cans (but supermarket wines carry *British* codes as they are labelled by the British distributor).

The *packet* containing a bottle of 'Tippex' correction fluid contains a West German code, and some Kodak film packets carry an American code. (Note: American *Universal Product Codes* are organised differently from EANs.)

Two pairs of thin black lines indicate the beginning and end of the code. A third pair also divides the code into two blocks. The bar codes for each digit are different on the left and right hand side of this division so that the computer 'knows' whether the code is being read right-to-left or left-to-right.

? **Q 5.11** Items not normally packaged could not easily be bar-coded (unless a special sticker was attached). Fresh fruit and vegetables, for example, are sold loose. Large consumer durables, e.g. sofas, cookers etc. are similarly not likely to be bar-coded. (Anyway, the turnover for furniture is slow and the stock-keeping problem would probably not justify such a sophisticated level of computing.)

? **Q 5.12** and **Q 5.13** The Post Office is obviously keen to use OCR as the basis for machine sorting of letters. The better equipped sorting offices already have OCR *automatic sorting machines* (ASMs) installed and these, typically, can sort eight letters per second, which is much faster than a human being could manage. However, the OCR machines have a very high rejection rate as addresses are often wrongly laid out (even the typewritten ones) and because handwriting varies so greatly. (The 'Cheltenham GL53 0DN' exercise is intended to illustrate this. Although a few people may be consistent and clear with their lettering, any class will contain a good number who are not.)

There are other problems, too. There is a Newcastle in Northern Ireland as well as in England. Fareham and Farnham are very similar names to machine sort (and the towns in question are only 35 miles apart so a nearby sorting office could have a lot of mail for both of them). Post codes greatly assist machine sorting.

Rejected letters are sorted manually.

? **Q 5.14** It would be sensible to object; a typist is bound to make errors if he or she is asked to type and retype meaningless lists of five letters. Some 'right' answers at key points (e.g. Q1) are likely to be learned by the typist and entered although they are not the candidate's actual answer and this sort of error may well be repeated by a second independent operator attempting to verify the input.

Without OMR, it is unlikely that examination authorities would have so readily taken to multiple choice testing.

? **Q 5.15** MICR is expensive. Banks depend on it though because of the security. It is difficult to tamper with magnetically encoded data. Shop systems are content with much cheaper OCR. Altering a bar code in order to pass off a large can of beans as a small one would not exactly justify the effort.

? **Q 5.16** The Phonecard encodes the number of unused phone credits and relays this information to the Cardphone as it is inserted (the Cardphone displays the number of credits left for the user's benefit).

Before the card is returned, the machine must alter the number of unused units left in order to take account of those used in the course of the current call.

? **Q 5.17** (*a*) Once the Cardphone is generally established the advantages will be:

(i) advance payment: at the moment, BT receives payment for the telephone service at the time of the call (in the case of a public telephone booth) or two or three months in arrears (in the case of a private telephone). The Cardphone system will cause people to pay for their telephone calls well in advance of making them.

(ii) security: many coin-boxes are vandalised and robbed of the money they contain. There is no point in trying to break into a Cardphone because there is no money inside.

(iii) ease of collection and variation of price: rather than employ staff to empty the coin-boxes, BT sells Phonecards at Post Offices. It follows that BT can vary the price of the card simply, too. At the moment BT increases prices by reducing the *time* bought for, say, a 10p coin. But there is a limit to this, and as inflation continues BT will one day have to modify its boxes (at some expense) to take £1 and even £2 coins.

(*b*) The customer has the advantage of:

(i) not having to worry about having the correct coinage for the call

(ii) calls not being interrupted by pips (unless the Phonecard is used up in the course of the call).

Both these considerations are especially important to travellers and business callers and the best places to see the Cardphone used are Heathrow, Gatwick, Manchester or Edinburgh Airports or at main-line railway terminals.

However, since 1986 BT have been installing very many more cardphones in Britain's high streets and many students will have seen (if not used) them.

? **Q 5.18** Many items now paid for by slot machine could easily be adapted to a magnetic charge card; e.g. launderettes, games machines, club facilities (such as squash-court lighting, sun-beds, showers etc.), gas and electricity in some homes, etc.

? **Q 5.19** The magnetically encoded, plastic National Insurance card was seen by some as the first move towards a unique machine-readable identity number by which all the computerised information held upon a particular individual could be readily accessed. For the same reason, some people are uneasy about the inclusion of a magnetic strip code on the new EEC passport due to be introduced in the UK (and already issued elsewhere in the Common Market).

? **Q 5.20** Chelsea was one of the first clubs to experiment with this idea; several clubs e.g. Reading adopted it in the 1985/86 season.

Their system depends upon portable card readers and supporters' club membership cards with photographs and magnetic strips. Not only does the system allow a club's authorities to know exactly who is at the match, it also opens up the possibility of matching faces in the crowd (misbehaviour is usually videotaped by the club or by the police) with the photographs collected when the cards were issued.

Other clubs have been resisting the idea (even after the Brussels disaster) not so much because of the expense, but more for fear that such a formalised system would drive away their considerable 'casual' trade, i.e. those fans who come only when the club is doing particularly well or is playing a famous opponent. Such fans would not bother to get club membership cards but would not be able to turn up on the day and watch the match without one.

So far, at least to the authors' knowledge, no one has suggested using the new machine-readable National Insurance card as a substitute club member's card. The NI card was not intended to act as an identity card and any suggestion that it might would, given the British tradition of not carrying such cards, stir huge political controversy.

On a more practical level, only a relatively small number of people (basically, those in their late teens, but then, *not* all 16-year-olds for some NI offices are still issuing their old cardboard stocks) have machine-readable plastic NI cards anyhow.

Discussion of these questions offers a useful opportunity to emphasise the importance of practical and political barriers to technological innovation.

? **Q 5.21** With a magnetic strip on every passport it should be possible to record the movements between states of every EEC national quickly and simply. Every entrant to the country could be checked against a 'Suspect Persons File' of those wanted for criminal offences (both in the UK and abroad) and of those (more sinisterly) regarded as 'undesirable' for other reasons. Forgery of passports would be a lot more difficult and it would be impossible for someone to travel within the EEC on a passport reported stolen.

The main drawback is that a very large proportion of travellers are nationals of countries outside the EEC and (without wider international agreements) they would not carry passports with codes (or at least with codes that could be read by the machinery at customs posts of the EEC). And a stolen EEC passport could be used successfully elsewhere in the world where it would not be electronically read.

? **Q 5.22** Punched cards are likely to disappear as an input method to most mainframe systems, although there are still many systems working effectively that have yet to be replaced.

The Kimball tag, on the other hand, will probably survive as a cheap means of collecting sales data at the point of sale for items such as clothes that could not be readily bar-coded.

Some simple clocking in and out mechanisms (such as at some car-parks) will probably continue to be punched card dependent too, because of the cost and complexity of alternatives.

EXERCISES 5

Q 5 (*a*) Although verification doubles the time (and hence cost) required to input data, it is *cheaper* than allowing inaccurate data to destroy the accuracy of the entire computer process (and so effectively waste the whole investment).

(*b*) Punched cards may no longer be a widespread means of data input, but the principles of key-to-tape and key-to-disk verification are very similar.

? **Q 13** Cassette tape; reel-to-reel tape; floppy disk; Winchester disk. Industrial systems are faster than 'home' alternatives; disks are faster than tapes.

? **Q 14** (*b*) Gas Boards and Electricity Boards are good examples. Meter readers fill in a mark sense card which is automatically read by an OMR device; so, other than the meter reader, human involvement is almost entirely eliminated from the billing process. The turnaround document must carry the account number (so that the consumer can be identified), the meter reading and the amount to be charged in a form suitable for OCR.

? **Q 16** Magnetically encoded cards are difficult to tamper with, and so they are ideal for this type of security. The number pad is necessary to allow the user to key in his PIN and so establish himself as the legitimate user. The computer validates the reading of the card (which should include its own check digit (see Chapter 11)), cross-checks the PIN and controls the opening of the door.

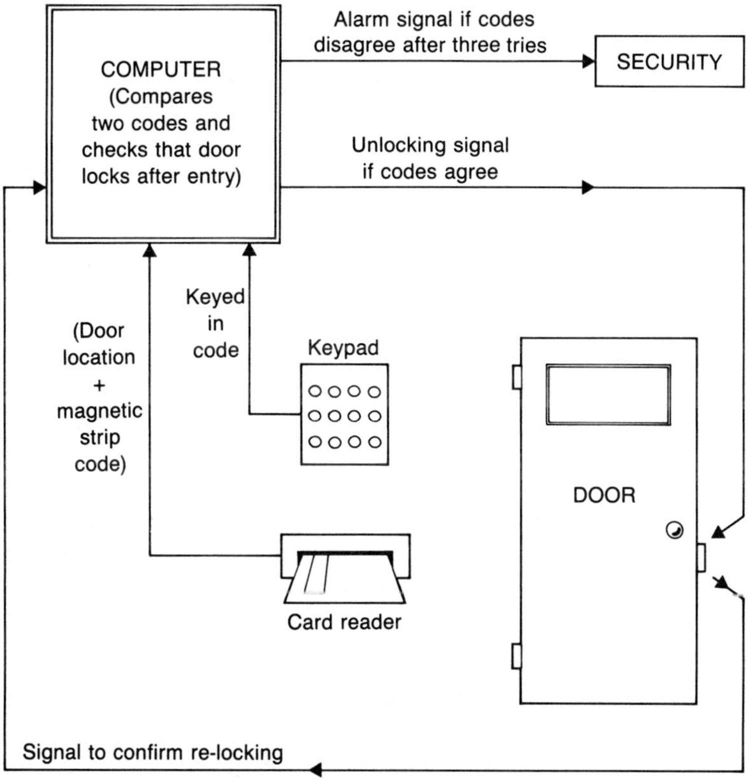

Fig. 5.2 Computer-controlled door system

Each door has its own card reader, activated by the insertion of the card. Each reader has a unique address code so that the computer can distinguish one location from another.

For multiple access, the system simply stores a table of authorised codes, users, doors and times:

Code	User	Doors accessible	Times
29067	Jones, A	1	any
		2	0700 - 2000
		3	no access
34561	Smith, J	1	no access
		2	0830 - 1830
		3	no access

When a card is inserted at one of the three doors, the computer compares the magnetically read code with that keyed in; it will check whether access is allowed at that door for that user and compare the times with its own clock before unlocking the door.

6 Output

DISCUSSION POINTS

? **Q 6.2** Computer operators working with VDUs for long stretches at a time must have as clear an image as possible to avoid eye strain. Debate continues as to whether prolonged VDU work has damaging effects beyond eye strain (e.g. from radiation). Research so far has not confirmed any such hazards. As with all sedentary work, back problems can result from poor posture at the terminal.

? **Q 6.3** (*a*) Any user of a microcomputer who would normally use it at the same desk; e.g. secretaries, authors, computer games players, businessmen, accountants, static managerial staff etc.

(*b*) Any user who is normally mobile, most obviously salespeople, building surveyors, warehousepeople, teachers (moving from one classroom to another or wanting to pass the same program around the class) etc.

Those whom we have put in group (*a*) would almost certainly find mobility an important plus, nonetheless.

? **Q 6.4** Different colours on TV are produced by blending the three primary colours, red, blue and green in different proportions and intensities. Each colour needs its own electron stream and deflectors.

? **Q 6.5** LCDs cannot be read in the dark unless specifically back-lit; LEDs can.

? **Q 6.6** LEDs absorb more power than LCDs and so tend not to be used on battery driven equipment (although this is not a hard-and-fast rule). However, the on/off lights in mains equipment are always LEDs so that the equipment may be clearly recognised as 'on', whatever the light-intensity of the surrounds; if the equipment is 'on' then the relatively small amount of power needed to drive the LED is readily available. Similarly, channel displays on TV and videos are usually LEDs to ensure that they can be seen in subdued light.

? **Q 6.7** Information stored electronically takes a fraction of the physical space (you might underline that idea by getting the class to work out the amount of paper needed to file the equivalent to a pack of ten double sided floppy disks; a page of A4 single-spaced typing takes up about 2 K) and can be readily sorted on a computer. However, people prefer to work on paper it seems; not least because it is the familiar medium. Portability, simplicity and security are also important factors.

? **Q 6.8** Any information outside a computer environment is generally conveyed verbally or in writing. Students will probably produce a wide variety of answers to this question. The words 'need to be' might be more strictly interpreted for cleverer classes: thus money transfers do not need to be by paper currency or cheque; electronic transfers are now fairly common (for monthly direct debits etc. see Chapter 17). Items that 'obviously' depend on paper, e.g. newspapers and books, might one day be distributed in forms different from those we know at present.

In general, items which (*a*) need to be recorded on a permanent or semi-permanent basis or (*b*) are intended to be read by those without compatible computer systems need to be in hard-copy form. Legal documents, for example, need to be on paper because the agreement needs to be a permanent record and a court of law would readily accept it on paper but probably not if the only record was an electronic one.

? **Q 6.9** Much of the information internal to a computerised organisation need not be printed out. For example, a school may keep information on courses, grades etc. of every student and may never need to print it out; similarly a business may keep track of day-to-day stock or profit levels and only print out an order or summary when appropriate. A lot of printing out is done for 'back-up' purposes, although, even when the information might be more readily stored and used on the computer system. Prudent businesses regularly make paper copies of important files.

It would be totally inappropriate to print out a lot of computerised information, e.g. the screen display at some instant of an interactive computer game or other simulation, or the moment by moment temperature of some computer controlled heat process.

? **Q 6.10** Even the cheapest electronic typewriters typically cost £200–£300 and the interface possibly another £50–£100. However, a computer hobbyist who may have only limited word-processing facilities on his home microcomputer might well prefer this arrangement to a computer printer. Obviously it gives him the choice of using the typewriter as a simple typewriter as well as a letter-quality printer for occasional computer output.

Students should understand, however, that the price difference is *now* small because of the fall in price of letter-quality printers; a few years ago an electronic typewriter and computer link would have been significantly cheaper.

? **Q 6.11** A typewriter is not an adequate substitute for a printer of professional quality, for it was not built to take the pounding of rapid computer printing speeds; it would be too slow for more than occasional use and be quickly worn out. Daisy-wheel typewriters work better than those of the golf-ball type (the golf-ball is a lot heavier than a plastic daisy-wheel) and were developed to replace the golf-ball machines for precisely this reason. The golf-ball typewriter was designed to replace the traditional individual-key systems because, at fast speeds, the keys would often collide and jam.

? **Q 6.12** It should not be possible to plug the wrong cable into a particular printer port because of the different shapes of plug. (This may provide an opportune moment to stress that students should never attempt to force a plug into a computer socket; there is likely to be a good reason for its not fitting.)

? **Q 6.13** Yes. Tractor feeds cost more than friction feed. Friction feeds, without a tractor option, are common at the cheap end of the daisy-wheel market (the printers are slow anyway). Any printer (but especially the faster ones) likely to be left unattended while it prints a file of some length needs a tractor system to keep the paper straight.

? **Q 6.14** Single sheets are preferable for formal letters (on headed notepaper for example). It is possible to attach a cut-sheet feeder to many printers, so that they can be left unattended. 'Up-market' continuous stationery, using tiny 'micro-perforations' (that are barely discernible once the sheets have been separated) and printed with a company's letter-heading is also available.

? **Q 6.15** and **6.16** Traditionally, typists' speeds assume an average word length of 5 characters (including spaces). Thus

$$40 \text{ w.p.m.} = \frac{40 \times 5}{60} = 3.3 \text{ c.p.s.}$$

Even the slowest daisy-wheel computer printer working at about 12 c.p.s. is typing at an equivalent of 144 w.p.m. A typical school-owned dot-matrix printer might print at 80 c.p.s. equivalent to 960 w.p.m.

According to the *Guinness Book of Records*, the world's fastest, sustained typing speed on an electric typewriter was set in 1941 by Margaret Hamma. She typed 9316 words in one hour, which, after penalties were imposed for the mistakes she made, was recorded as 149 w.p.m. – just slightly faster (by five words per minute) than the *slowest* daisy-wheel printer.

It would have taken Miss Hamma well over two minutes to type page 110 of the main book. It would take a computer printer working at 100 c.p.s. just 16 seconds.

? **Q 6.17** Thermal printers are generally the cheapest.

? **Q 6.18** Once.

? **Q 6.20** Ink-jet printers can produce colour fairly easily. (Of course it is possible to fit a colour ribbon onto a dot-matrix printer; but only a few models can organise several interwoven colours on one document, using a multi-coloured ribbon.)

They can also print onto awkward surfaces. For example, the 'best-before' date on the bottom of a drinks can (mentioned in the text) is a difficult printing job because the surface is of nonporous metal and is often an odd concave shape. Obviously, the metal surface will necessitate a careful choice of ink but otherwise the task is routine for an ink-jet printer.

? **Q 6.21** Generally ink-jet printers work best on porous papers. The print on high-quality 'shiny' papers is prone to smudge and run. The ink used needs to be of good quality, to prevent the fine jets from clogging up.

? **Q 6.22** Hewlett Packard's Laserjet and Apple's Laserwriter retail at under £3000. The cheapest laser printers have broken the £2000 barrier (December 1986).

? **Q 6.23** Old newspapers and so on take up a great deal of storage space and discolour and deteriorate surprisingly quickly. Microfilm is compact and does not deteriorate.

? **Q 6.25** Voice output is not simply a gimmick, although some of the uses to which it is put may well be. For example, there are 'speaking' coffee machines and electric irons.

Audible warnings for, say, seatbelts are more likely to be noticed than are warning lights. As important, the computer could be programmed to signal a wide variety of potential problems without surrounding the driver with a large and confusing array of warning lights. The same goes for aircraft pilots whose instruments are becoming even more complex.

The 'speak' of the Texas Instruments 'Speak 'n' Spell' is crucial to setting the child the problem and to his or her learning as the word is keyed in.

There are machines that speak on behalf of disabled people who cannot voice intelligibly for themselves and other machines that use OCR and voice synthesis to 'read' books to the blind.

As the technology improves, so voice output and input will grow to tremendous importance. Computer users will not be tied to a desk, typing their input and reading output on a VDU or printer. Instead they will be able to converse with a new (fifth) generation of computers that can talk to them and vice versa.

7 Storage

DISCUSSION POINTS

? **Q 7.1** Every computer must have an operating system (if only simple 'loader' software which merely loads other operating systems such as CP/M or MS-DOS).

? **Q 7.2** Both PROM and EPROM offer the user greater flexibility than simple ROM, fixed for life by the manufacturer. However, only specialist users can program these chips, for fairly costly machinery is involved.

? **Q 7.3** *Advantages:* non-volatile RAM enables truly portable computers capable of storing, say, a 30-page document without disk storage. It also enables the computer to remember the correct date and time.

Powered RAM is most suitable for hostile environments (say, a dusty building site) as the computer can be sealed against the elements unlike a disk-drive.

Disadvantages: batteries will need replacing from time to time. It may be harder to transfer data from one machine to another and, similarly, making back-ups could be more difficult. Powered RAM necessarily limits the volume of possible storage (which is limitless with removable disks).

? **Q 7.4** If a large file such as that suggested could be stored in main memory on a permanent basis, then the file would be that much easier to use and that much faster to alter. However, there would still be the need for back-up copies, in case the file is inadvertently lost.

The file might be more susceptible to unauthorised access.

Perhaps the most important disadvantage would be that the computer would be permanently filled with information from one single file and could not then be used for much else. It would become dedicated to the one application.

Of course, the question is academic at the moment, because such a file in RAM would automatically be lost as soon as the machine was turned off.

? **Q 7.5** The number of uses for a machine without backing store are very limited. It would only be possible to run those programs which the user was prepared to type in himself, and so the machine could not be used for complex games and educational programs. Nor would it be possible to use the computer as a file for telephone numbers, recipes etc. Word processing of sorts would be possible, although one of the greatest assets of a WP system, namely being able to revise and up-date documents in the long term, would be lost.

? **Q 7.6** No; *t*, *i* and *c* are all wrong.

? **Q 7.7** Odd parity ensures an odd number of spots in each frame.

? **Q 7.8** A parity check is not fool-proof for it is possible that *two* bits would be misread, in which case the errors will self-cancel and the parity will appear to be correct.

? **Q 7.9** Depends on your system. But note that the straightforward techniques outlined in the text might be replaced by so-called 'perpendicular recording' that uses the vertical dimension as well as the horizontal. This may increase the capacity of a $5\frac{1}{4}$ in floppy to as much as 20 megabytes.

? **Q 7.10** It is easier to make (essential) back-up copies with a dual disk drive than with a single drive. Most mainframes have a number of disk drives attached and use tape units for making back-up copies. Tapes are cheaper than disks and problems of serial versus direct access do not apply if the tapes will only be used in an emergency. Disk packs can be bulkier than reels of tape.

? **Q 7.11** The write-protect notch will be in the wrong place.

? **Q 7.12** Because the computing industry is led by American companies (such as IBM).

The first 'Winchester' (hard) disk system was a dual disk drive with 30 megabytes of storage in each drive. This 30–30 capacity was responsible for the name, after the famous Winchester 30–30 rifle.

? **Q 7.13** Any real-time application in which the computer must decide how to respond to an event quickly enough to effect its outcome cannot tolerate delay. Many non-urgent uses of a computer, e.g. word processing for example, would soon become tedious if there were several minutes delay every time the backing store was used.

? **Q 7.14** A basic cheap cassette deck of a quality sufficient for a home computer costs about £20. C30 tapes cost a little less than £1. A C15 tape can be bought for 50p.

A basic, single-sided 40-track disk drive for, say, the BBC costs about £80 for the cheapest, excluding leads. The disks cost around £1.20 each; i.e. £12 for a box of ten. (All prices for January 1987.)

? **Q 7.15** Video tape recorders work by recording electromagnetic signals off-air; they are read/write mechanisms. So far, laser based video disks* are read-only mechanisms; the public has not taken to them because people do not want to watch repeated showings of the same TV programme with the possible exception of pop-music 'videos' (i.e. video recordings).

On the other hand, people do like to listen again and again to a piece of music, and the read-only nature of an audio compact disc is not a handicap (an ordinary gramophone record is, of course, a read-only device).

? **Q 7.16** Any archival use is suitable for read-only backing store. In fact many records held on magnetic read/write media are rendered read-only by appropriate adjustment of the write-protect notch. This is not only done in a computing context; cassette tapes and video tapes are often similarly protected.

Read/write laser disks will be commonplace by the end of the decade. The American floppy disk company Verbatim has produced a 3 in read/write optical disk with 40 megabytes capacity, and expects to mass produce it by 1988. Other companies have devised similar products.

*Following the style of 'programme' and 'program' we have retained the English spelling of the word 'disc' whenever it is used in the context of home entertainment and (following the British Computer Society's recommendation) we have used the American spelling 'disk' in the context of a computer system. As laser disks are increasingly important in computing, we have used 'k'.

Part C Information Systems

8 Types of System

DISCUSSION POINTS

? **Q 8.1** *Example* A home computer with 256 K RAM has capacity for 256×1024 characters. If there are (approx) 2000 characters per page,

$$\text{number of pages} = \frac{256 \times 1024}{2000} \approx 131 \text{ pages of book.}$$

? **Q 8.2** (*a*) A 'stand alone' microcomputer offers low cost, no complications with other users accessing and/or amending files, no waiting time for others to clear computer or peripherals (e.g. a shared printer), and a vast range of inexpensive software available.

(*b*) A mainframe terminal offers easy access to central files and the vast power of the mainframe. But telephone links can be unreliable and remote processing on a mainframe is generally expensive.

? **Q 8.3** Many commercial organisations would rather use a mainframe than many micros. The better known applications that should be mentioned are NASA, weather forecasters, Inland Revenue, DHSS, local authorities etc.

? **Q 8.4** The likelihood is that some minicomputers will be crowded out; a number of minicomputer manufacturers have already gone out of business. However, other companies have enjoyed so successful a *software* track record that they might well survive.

? **Q 8.5** Interaction is the key to successful home computing. It is likely that most students will have nothing left on their lists.

? **Q 8.6** A second's delay would be too long in most process control applications. For example, Fig. 8.14 in the main text shows a computer controlling sugar flow from an overhead hopper. If the valve consistently closed one second too late, then the mixture would be consistently over-sweetened. (Countermeasures are possible but this should make the point clear.)

? **Q 8.7** On-line systems need *not* be real-time. For example, a terminal may be on-line for, say, one hour per day in order to process a batch of data. It is clearly not a real-time system. But real-time systems *are*, of necessity, on-line.

? **Q 8.8** (*a*) The automatic sprinkler responds as soon as it senses the fire and its reaction will douse the fire. The event (the fire) generates the response (sprinkling) fast enough for the event itself to be affected. So this is both on-line *and* real-time.

(*b*) The computer is on-line, but the response is delayed (perhaps the firemen are out at another fire) so it is *not* real-time.

(*c*) Neither. The watchman is 'off-line' when he first notices the fire.

? **Q 8.9**

	(*a*) time sharing	(*b*) multi-access	(*c*) multiprogramming
(i)	×	×	×
(ii)	✓	✓	✓
(iii)	✓	✓	×
(iv)	✓	✓	×
(v)	✓	×	✓

Notes: Some Prestel users are extracting information, others are downloading computer programs, some are feeding information into the system; thus a variety of users are requiring different programs.

The space shuttle computer is *not* multi-access if we assume only *one* astronaut has responsibility for checking its output.

? **Q 8.10** *Cost:* This question offers an ideal opportunity to explain your school/college computer network, the cost of the system etc. Stress that the hardware and software required to make a LAN work is itself expensive.

? **Q 8.11** *Multi-users:* There are many advantages, e.g. demonstration programs, debugging exercises and team program drafting. The main disadvantage is that one user could overwrite another's file by choosing the same file name.

? **Q 8.12** The head teacher's files will necessarily maintain a good deal of confidential information about students and staff that should never become common knowledge. The security of computerised files is discussed later (Chapter 11). It should be possible for the head teacher to use the network *and* protect the files with several passwords and codes.

EXERCISES 8

Q 4 Mainframes will not disappear, but will continue to increase in power.

9 Developing Systems

Developing a computer system involves many stages, and the computer itself is not involved much of the time. Students must understand that programming is only one small phase in the complete systems development cycle.

DISCUSSION POINTS

? **Q 9.1** Some suggestions: the motorway system, the signalling system for traffic lights (increasingly computerised), the braking system on a car (an anti-locking brake system is controlled by a chip), the parliamentary system, the 'totting-up' penalty points system for endorsing driving licences, the GCSE examination system, the telephone system (only partly computerised), a crop rotation system for farmers, the system for calculating dividends on the football pools (the pools companies are extensively computerised), notation systems (e.g. music, knitting patterns), any language (natural or computer) and payroll systems (manual or computerised).

? **Q 9.2** Many home and school computer users have attempted to computerise:

Address books: But there is little point because of the risk of data loss, and the inconvenience in use.

Recipes: The above applies.

Telephone directories: These are more debatable, as they could possibly be effective if all directories were computerised and all subscribers had a terminal on which to make directory enquiries. Autodialing could be useful for frequent telephone users.

Daily school register: It is probably pointless to computerise this unless the school plans a daily absentees list.

School timetables: There are so many variables that they are very difficult to computerise effectively. However, schools are gradually moving to automated timetabling.

Diaries: These are not usually worth the effort for one person, but can be effective for organisations that use substantial office automation. Colleagues can book provisional meetings in each other's diaries without needing to speak. This (like an ordinary diary) requires discipline to remember to keep it up to date and to consult it regularly. People would need portable (preferably pocket-sized) terminals to make this sytem fully effective.

? **Q 9.3** Problems include:

Conflicting accounts of how the system works; key people being absent or too busy to see the analyst; hostility or suspicion; being accidentally or deliberately misled; getting sidetracked and wasting time on subjects not relevant to the investigation; documents or files missing; users who want to design or instal a new system before the study is complete.

? **Q 9.4** We suggest that students do this exercise in writing, with a limit of, say, half a page to complete the description. See whether other students can understand, let alone perform, the jobs from the descriptions alone.

? **Q 9.5** The first objective can be achieved by simply having enough people to answer the telephones, although a computerised switchboard may help to minimise delays in switching calls through to the right person. Staff can be trained to deal with customers courteously yet promptly. The speed with which required information can be obtained will of course affect the length of each call.

Finding out within 15 seconds whether an item is in stock would be impossible without computer assistance.

Dealing with complaints within 24 hours would be much easier with a well designed computer system, but success would still depend very much on staff determination to clear up outstanding queries and problems; the computer will not do it for them.

? **Q 9.6** The relatively small investment (in time and money) for a feasibility study can be very worthwhile. It can save expensive mistakes, such as launching an ambitious development project which could never be cost-effective, or it can uncover an opportunity which would otherwise have been missed.

? **Q 9.7** Possible contents:

Customer name
Initials
Title (Mr, Mrs, Ms, Miss)
Customer address
Telephone number
Account number
Account type (cash/credit, weekly/monthly)

Balance owing

Payment amount(s) (could be many items as customers can purchase a number of goods *each* on an instalment basis)

Goods purchased (probably linked to payment amounts)

Payment history (chronically poor payers must be monitored)

Credit rating

Credit limit

Outstanding orders

Goods returned (to check that the customer is not sending back too many items)

Agency details (if customer also acts as an agent).

? **Q 9.8** Internal data examples: Stock number, quantity in stock, supplier details, re-order level (e.g. re-order when only one dozen left), re-order quantity (e.g. order six dozen of each size), cost price, delivery time etc.

External data examples: Customer's size(s), method of payment, bank account/credit-card numbers if needed, whether or not customer has received latest catalogue.

? **Q 9.9** There is no *right way* to design a form; Fig. 9.1 (overleaf) is a suggestion, on which readers may be able to improve.

? **Q 9.10** A store cupboard, e.g. a larder at home, a stationery cupboard at school. A sweet shop. A gasometer. In each case, a rapid visual check will determine which items are low or out of stock.

? **Q 9.11** Simply by using English prompts and messages rather than computer mumbo-jumbo. The user is given virtually no idea what to key in, and has to remember awkward, obscure command formats.

? **Q 9.12** It is again worth getting students to test these instructions out on each other, with no assistance or clues allowed except the program and the written instructions.

? **Q 9.13** Unless the system configurations (hardware and software) are very similar, it is not an easy task to transfer production jobs (i.e. normal day-to-day processing) between installations. There is also a real danger of disrupting the systems of the host installation by dramatically increasing the workload of its machine(s). Rehearsals would be advisable for any such contingency plan.

? **Q 9.14** Refer to our six rules of good computer programming on page 51 of the main text.

? **Q 9.15** (*a*) The old sales details and old outstanding orders files are both input to the computer; the new versions are output. The stock master file and the customer master file are both input and output files as they are both accessed for information and updated continually as processing proceeds.

JILL TAYLOR MAIL ORDER PLC **ORDER/ENQUIRY FORM** **SERIAL NO.**

Time ☐ am/pm Date ☐ Employee Name ☐ Dept. ☐

Customer Surname ☐ Initials ☐ Mr/Mrs/Miss/Ms

Address ☐

Post Code ☐

Telephone: Exchange ☐ Code ☐ Number ☐

Existing Customer? Yes/No If so, JT Account Number ☐

Has Current Catalogue? Yes/No JT Agent? Yes/No

Description of Item(s)	Catalogue Number	Size	Colour	Order Qty.	Paymt. Method	Enqy.	Compt.

Other Comments ☐ Other Enquiry ☐ Complaint ☐ (explain below)

Order Actions

Stock Alloc.

Credit Check ☐ Time ☐ am/pm Date ☐ Initials ☐

Pass to Despatch ☐ Time ☐ am/pm Date ☐ Initials ☐

Copy to Accounts ☐ Time ☐ am/pm Date ☐ Initials ☐

Other Action (specify)

Time ☐ am/pm Date ☐ Initials ☐

Enquiry Followup

Action Taken

Time ☐ am/pm Date ☐ Initials ☐

Complaint Followup

Action Taken

Time ☐ am/pm Date ☐ Initials ☐

Passed to Supervisor ☐ Time ☐ am/pm Date ☐ Initials ☐

Further Action

Time ☐ am/pm Date ☐ Initials ☐

Fig. 9.1 A possible order/inquiry form

Customers' orders are keyed in individually as they are received, so are not gathered together as an input file. Remind students that printed reports (sales analyses, outstanding orders, customer bills and warehouse lists) are all output files.

(*b*) The arrows indicate information flows: double heads are shown for files that are updated-in-place (e.g. the stock master file) and single heads for files that are simply input (e.g. the old outstanding orders file) or simply output (e.g. printed reports). Orders are keyed in at the VDU, but the update program also sends information (about customers, stock etc.) back to the operator's screen.

(*c*) Nearly all mail order companies require rapid response to stock enquiries and immediate processing and despatch of orders. Batch systems simply cannot provide this.

(*d*) All files will be on disk (probably hard disk, because of the volume) except, of course, the print files which will be output to standard pre-printed stationery.

(*e*) (i) Will be used by the accountants operating the sales ledger system. (ii) Any order which cannot be met from stock will be placed on this file, which is checked whenever goods received from suppliers are entered onto the stock master file. (iii) The warehouse lists (also called 'picking lists') enable the warehouse staff to select and pack the correct goods for dispatch to customers.

? **Q 9.16** A company must know, for every sale it has made, whether or not it has been paid. This is a central function of a sales ledger system.

? **Q 9.17** Generally, software companies who hope to sell hundreds or thousands of copies of a software product will take more time and trouble over its design and testing than for a one-off sale of custom-built software. They can spread the cost of such thorough testing (which might be prohibitive for a single client) over all their customers and the price can still be reasonable.

On the other hand, small software houses often operate on shoestring budgets and simply cannot afford such a thorough approach. Furthermore, amendments to packages are sometimes rushed through with inadequate design and testing, in order that existing users of the package can receive the new version quickly.

10 Files

Students at all levels tend to find files confusing. Many find the distinction between fields, records and files difficult, and so it is worth spending extra time with examples and manual/computer parallels in order to reinforce the definitions.

File structure, in particular, is a minefield. We have tried to make it as simple as possible by describing only the three *main* types of file organisation method: sequential (or serial), indexed and direct. Teachers should be aware that the text deliberately omits several points that are too complex for this level. Especially able groups, or those beyond 16 + , may wish to delve deeper.

No distinction has been made between serial and sequential files. Strictly, the former store records in no particular order while the latter store them in a predetermined sequence, usually key sequence. In practice such a sequence is nearly always used and even unsorted (serial) files are commonly called 'sequential'.

Similarly the British Computer Society defines sequential (serial) access as 'the process of storing or retrieving data items by first reading through all previous items to locate the one required'. We have implied that this is *the usual* way to access sequential files, ignoring the (relatively rare) cases where other methods, such as binary searching, can be used.

We have implied that updating a sequential file generally involves creating a whole new version of the file. Strictly, there are exceptions to this: *some* systems in *some* circumstances enable updating-in-place of *some* sequential files. To discuss these (again, rare) cases is beyond the scope of this book. The generalisation is, we feel, justified for the sake of clarity.

No mention is made in the text of relative files (in which the key value represents the record position relative to the start of the file). Relative files are unlikely to be used at this level.

Finally, we have not distinguished fully indexed files from indexed sequential files (which can be accessed via an index *or* sequentially); this is also too advanced.

WORKSHEETS

The ideas underlying the filing process as described in the pupils' text are *not* really as difficult as they seem on first reading. We hope that the *Updating The Master File Exercise* that follows will help.

It is intended that you should photocopy the exercise instructions, *The Endangered Species Master File Worksheet* and the *Transaction Files Worksheet* (pp 46–8) and allow each student to have a copy of each.

The successive updates should be completed in different colours on the one Endangered Species Master by writing the amendments in the blank lines above each record in the file.

Answer sheets are enclosed. You might use photocopies of these to explain in concrete terms the workings of the Ancestral Files System.

The following may help to make sure students understand clearly the ponderous, step-by-step nature of updating the files.

Amendments

Step 1: Read first transaction key (= 00010)
Step 2: Read records from old master; copy *one-by-one* to new master until key = 00010
Step 3: Amend record and write to new master
Step 4: Read next transaction key (= 00030)
Step 5: Read records from old master: copy to new until key = 00030
Step 6: Change this record as instructed . . . and so on until end of old master is reached

Insertions

The update described above processed only *amendment* transactions. To - *insert* one new record into an ordinary sequential file, the program must carry out four steps:

Step 1: Read the key of the record to be inserted, storing the record details in main memory
Step 2: Read and copy all records *with keys less than the insertion key* from the old file to the new file
Step 3: Write the new record from memory to the new file
Step 4: Read and copy all records *with keys greater than the insertion key* from the old file to the new file.

Deletions

The procedure for deleting a single record is similar:

Step 1: Read (and store in main memory) the key of the record to be deleted
Step 2: Read and copy all records *with keys less than the deletion key* from the old file to the new file
Step 3: *Ignore* the record on the old file whose key matches the deletion key; this is the one to be deleted
Step 4: Read and copy all records *with keys greater than the deletion key* from the old file to the new file.

The update program will provide for errors—so the operator cannot insert a new record with a key field the same as an existing record, amend a non-existent record, or similar.

EXERCISE: UPDATING THE MASTER FILE

For this you will need a copy of *The Endangered Species Master File Worksheet* and a copy of the *Transaction Files Worksheet* that will be used to update it.

First Update

Imagine that you are the computer used to update the Master File, given Transaction File 1.

Assume that not only is the file sequential, but also that only *sequential* access is possible, because the files are held on tape. You must read each file record by record to find the one you want.

You cannot go back to an earlier record

Remember also that

Transaction Code **A**	means	**A**mend the specified record
Transaction Code **D**	means	**D**elete the specified record
Transaction Code **I**	means	**I**nsert a new record (which will be held in the transaction file with a structure identical to that of the Master)

Second Update

(a) Try to amend the Master File using the unsorted Transaction File 2A. Remember that the files allow sequential access only. What happens?

(b) Sort the Transaction File 2A, rewriting it into a sorted file, 2B. Now update the Master File for the second time.

Third Update

Now assume that the Master File has been transferred to disk and that you now have *direct* access to every record in the Master File.

Use Transaction File 3 to update the Master File for the third time. Why has direct access to each record made the third update much simpler than the second?

Use the series of amended files to explain the **Ancestral files system**. Which of your files are the **Grandfather**, the **Father** and the **Son** Files?

Worksheets Transaction Files

TRANSACTION FILE 1

Transaction Code	Reference Number	Transaction Details
A	00010	MINPOP=850
D	00030	
A	00040	MAINLOC=BRAZIL
A	00090	MAXPOP=150
D	00100	
I	00105	NUBIAN WILD ASS NORTH EAST SUDAN 0000000050

TRANSACTION FILE 2A

Transaction Code	Reference Number	Transaction Details
A	00150	MAXPOP=20
A	00010	MAINLOC=ANTARCTIC SEAS
D	00110	
A	00070	MINPOP=60
I	00030	GIANT OTTER EAST BRAZIL 0004000500

TRANSACTION FILE 2B (SORTED ON REFERENCE NUMBER)

Transaction Code	Reference Number	Transaction Details

TRANSACTION FILE 3

Transaction Code	Reference Number	Transaction Details
A	00140	MAINLOC=BURMA
A	00020	MAXPOP=100
D	00150	
I	00055	MCNEILL'S DEER TIBET 0000000040
A	00130	MINPOP=250

REF NUMBER	NAME OF ANIMAL	MAIN LOCATION	POPULATION MIN	POPULATION MAX
00010	BLUE WHALE	ANTARCTIC REGION	00700	02000
00020	BRANDERS SWAMP DEER	MADHYA PREDESH, INDIA	00050	00090
00030	CARIBBEAN MONK SEAL	CARIBBEAN ISLANDS	00000	00050
00040	GOLDEN LION MARMOSET	SOUTH EAST BRAZIL	00400	00600
00050	JAVAN RHINOCEROS	JAVA	00010	00060
00060	MEDITERRANEAN MONK SEAL	MEDITERRANEAN	00300	00600
00070	MEXICAN GRIZZLY BEAR	SIERRA MADRE, MEXICO	00030	00100
00080	NORTHERN KIT FOX	SASKATCHEWAN, CANADA	00000	00050
00090	NORTHERN SQUARE-LIPPED RHINOCEROS	UGANDA	00025	00100
00100	NOVAYA ZEMLYA REINDEER	NOVAYA ZEMLYA, USSR	00020	00075
00110	RED WOLF	TEXAS, USA	00000	00040
00120	SAN JOAQUIN FOX	NEW MEXICO, USA	00150	00600
00130	SOMALI WILD ASS	ETHIOPIA	00400	00800
00140	SUMATRAN RHINOCEROS	SUMATRA	00100	00175
00150	WOOLLY SPIDER MONKEY	SOUTH EAST BRAZIL	00000	00100

ENDANGERED SPECIES MASTER FILE

REF NUMBER	NAME OF ANIMAL	MAIN LOCATION	POPULATION MIN	POPULATION MAX
00010	BLUE WHALE	ANTARCTIC REGION	00850	02000
00020	BRANDERS SWAMP DEER	MADHYA PREDESH, INDIA	00050	00090
00040	GOLDEN LION MARMOSET	BRAZIL	00400	00600
00050	JAVAN RHINOCEROS	JAVA	00010	00060
00060	MEDITERRANEAN MONK SEAL	MEDITERRANEAN	00300	00600
00070	MEXICAN GRIZZLY BEAR	SIERRA MADRE, MEXICO	00030	00100
00080	NORTHERN KIT FOX	SASKATCHEWAN, CANADA	00000	00050
00090	NORTHERN SQUARE-LIPPED RHINOCEROS	UGANDA	00025	00150
00105	NUBIAN WILD ASS	NORTH EAST SUDAN	00000	00050
00110	RED WOLF	TEXAS, USA	00000	00040
00120	SAN JOAQUIN FOX	NEW MEXICO, USA	00150	00600
00130	SOMALI WILD ASS	ETHIOPIA	00400	00800
00140	SUMATRAN RHINOCEROS	SUMATRA	00100	00175
00150	WOOLLY SPIDER MONKEY	SOUTH EAST BRAZIL	00000	00100

ENDANGERED SPECIES MASTER FILE AFTER UPDATE 1

REF NUMBER	NAME OF ANIMAL	MAIN LOCATION	POPULATION MIN	POPULATION MAX
00010	BLUE WHALE	ANTARCTIC REGION	00850	02000
00020	BRANDERS SWAMP DEER	MADHYA PREDESH, INDIA	00050	00090
00040	GOLDEN LION MARMOSET	BRAZIL	00400	00600
00050	JAVAN RHINOCEROS	JAVA	00010	00060
00060	MEDITERRANEAN MONK SEAL	MEDITERRANEAN	00300	00600
00070	MEXICAN GRIZZLY BEAR	SIERRA MADRE, MEXICO	00030	00100
00080	NORTHERN KIT FOX	SASKATCHEWAN, CANADA	00000	00050
00090	NORTHERN SQUARE-LIPPED RHINOCEROS	UGANDA	00025	00150
00105	NUBIAN WILD ASS	NORTH EAST SUDAN	00000	00050
00110	RED WOLF	TEXAS, USA	00000	00040
00120	SAN JOAQUIN FOX	NEW MEXICO, USA	00150	00600
00130	SOMALI WILD ASS	ETHIOPIA	00400	00800
00140	SUMATRAN RHINOCEROS	SUMATRA	00100	00175
00150	WOOLLY SPIDER MONKEY	SOUTH EAST BRAZIL	00000	00020

ENDANGERED SPECIES MASTER FILE AFTER UPDATE 2A

REF NUMBER	NAME OF ANIMAL	MAIN LOCATION	POPULATION MIN	POPULATION MAX
00010	BLUE WHALE	ANTARCTIC SEAS	00850	02000
00020	BRANDERS SWAMP DEER	MADHYA PREDESH, INDIA	00050	00090
00030	GIANT OTTER	EAST BRAZIL	00040	00050
00040	GOLDEN LION MARMOSET	BRAZIL	00400	00600
00050	JAVAN RHINOCEROS	JAVA	00010	00060
00060	MEDITERRANEAN MONK SEAL	MEDITERRANEAN	00300	00600
00070	MEXICAN GRIZZLY BEAR	SIERRA MADRE, MEXICO	00060	00100
00080	NORTHERN KIT FOX	SASKATCHEWAN, CANADA	00000	00050
00090	NORTHERN SQUARE-LIPPED RHINOCEROS	UGANDA	00025	00150
00105	NUBIAN WILD ASS	NORTH EAST SUDAN	00000	00050
00120	SAN JOAQUIN FOX	NEW MEXICO, USA	00150	00600
00130	SOMALI WILD ASS	ETHIOPIA	00400	00800
00140	SUMATRAN RHINOCEROS	SUMATRA	00100	00175
00150	WOOLLY SPIDER MONKEY	SOUTH EAST BRAZIL	00000	00020

ENDANGERED SPECIES MASTER FILE AFTER UPDATE 2B

REF NUMBER	NAME OF ANIMAL	MAIN LOCATION	POPULATION MIN	POPULATION MAX
00010	BLUE WHALE	ANTARCTIC SEAS	00850	02000
00020	BRANDERS SWAMP DEER	MADHYA PREDESH, INDIA	00050	00100
00030	GIANT OTTER	EAST BRAZIL	00040	00050
00040	GOLDEN LION MARMOSET	BRAZIL	00400	00600
00050	JAVAN RHINOCEROS	JAVA	00010	00060
00055	MCNEILL'S DEER	TIBET	00000	00040
00060	MEDITERRANEAN MONK SEAL	MEDITERRANEAN	00300	00600
00070	MEXICAN GRIZZLY BEAR	SIERRA MADRE, MEXICO	00060	00100
00080	NORTHERN KIT FOX	SASKATCHEWAN, CANADA	00000	00050
00090	NORTHERN SQUARE-LIPPED RHINOCEROS	UGANDA	00025	00150
00105	NUBIAN WILD ASS	NORTH EAST SUDAN	00000	00050
00120	SAN JOAQUIN FOX	NEW MEXICO, USA	00150	00600
00130	SOMALI WILD ASS	ETHIOPIA	00250	00800
00140	SUMATRAN RHINOCEROS	BURMA	00100	00175

ENDANGERED SPECIES MASTER FILE AFTER UPDATE 3

DISCUSSION POINTS

? **Q 10.1** Common examples include address and telephone books, recipe books, savings books, other 'accounts' files (bank, building society etc.), lists for sending Christmas cards or buying presents, household inventories (such as might be made when insuring contents). Even a simple shopping list can be regarded as a file, each record representing something which must be bought, e.g. eggs. Sometimes the records may be more complex, showing quantity, quality etc. (e.g. 12 size 3 free-range eggs).

It may seem obvious, but to manage information effectively it is not enough merely to store it somewhere. We must know where it is stored, in what form and how it can be accessed if it is to be of any use. A friend's telephone number is useless if you 'stored' it on the back of an envelope and forgot to transfer it to your address book. Mrs Beeton's Christmas pudding recipe is awkward to use if your kitchen scales are marked for metric weights only. And how often have you forgotten to take your shopping list to the supermarket?

? **Q 10.2** Most students will have used a home computer, in which case the most common files they will have encountered are those storing programs, including games. The medium may be cassette, disk or chip, and each record is a machine code statement (or data) for a specific game. Other computer files may of course have been used at school or college, but two more common examples are:

- On-line store or supermarket stock files, or any store using bar codes at the checkouts. The storage medium is usually hard disk and each record holds details of one stock item sold in the store.
- Bank or building society cashcard customer files. Any cash dispensing machine must be able to check a customer file (usually also a disk file) before issuing cash.

? **Q 10.3** Single-character fields are quite common, e.g. personnel records often have a field containing 'M' or 'F' to indicate male or female employees. Other records may include single-character 'flags' or indicator fields containing 'Y' or 'N' (for yes or no); this could mean 'out of stock', 'on order', 'existing customer', 'active account' etc.

Records are usually made up from several fields, but this is not essential. A letter stored on disk via a word processing program might contain 80-character records, each holding one line of text.

There would be no point in breaking down such records into smaller fields, as the letter would be accessed line by line.

? **Q 10.4** A similar exercise appears earlier in the text, but one is included here because some students have a persistent misconception. They imagine that *somehow* a computer can 'remember' entire files, irrespective of their size. It is not obvious that files are normally processed one record at a time. If a record is read from a file into the same area of main memory as the previous record, that previous record is no longer available to the program—unless the programmer has taken the trouble to store it elsewhere.

Space required = 800 × 300 × 64 = 15 360 000 bytes. The space in one 256 K computer RAM = 256 × 1024 = 262 144 bytes. Therefore the number of computers needed = 15 360 000/262 144 = 58.59, i.e. 59 computers. Note that 1 K = 2^{10} = 1024, and that in practice most '256 K' machines give the user less *available* RAM, so 59 machines would not suffice.

? **Q 10.5** Whether printing, updating or just examining a file, it is vital to be able to separate fields. For example, it is difficult to get much meaning from this record:

06294ACMEENGINEERINGLTD.   03347463320005000000400000H

until you know that:

- characters 1–5 represent account number,
- characters 6–35 represent customer name,
- characters 36–45 represent telephone number,
- characters 46–53 represent balance owing (pence),
- characters 54–61 represent credit limit (pence), and
- character 62 represents H(ome) or E(xport).

? **Q 10.6** It is a chore to enter lengthy key fields. Moreover, it is hard to key in, say, 'Toot-Ee Froot-Ee Ices & Desserts Ltd.' in exactly the same way each time. Having over-long keys also reduces access speed, especially when using indexed files.

? **Q 10.7** With a four-digit key, 10 000 species could be uniquely identified (0000 to 9999) using *decimal digits* only. If, however, the letters A–Z were also used, instead of a limit of (10 × 10 × 10 × 10) we could store (36 × 36 × 36 × 36) or 1 679 616 different species.

? **Q 10.8** For your particular class, surnames might suffice to identify each student uniquely. But duplicate surnames often do occur, and so it would be wise to use initials and surname together as the key. A unique student number could be used, but of course you would need to know somehow that Molesworth, N. was in fact 0175.

Using the name as a key is possible also for the customer record, but as customer names could easily be up to 40 characters long, access might be laborious. So most systems will resort to a unique customer code (see ACME Engineering above). Again you would need some way of looking up the appropriate account number, which is tiresome. Some systems allow a hybrid account number, such as ACME00. This is easy to remember, quick to key in, and allows addition of, say, ACME Microcomputers Ltd. as customer number ACME10.

Q 10.9 Students' efforts will vary considerably. Our suggested answer (just one of many possible solutions) is:

FAMILY NAME	C	30
OTHER NAMES	C	30
ADDRESS LINE 1	C	25
ADDRESS LINE 2	C	25
ADDRESS LINE 3	C	25
ADDRESS LINE 4	C	25
POSTCODE	C	9
TELEPHONE NUMBER	C	18

NB 'C' means character field, i.e. alphanumeric as opposed to numeric.

For some addresses, 4 × 25 characters plus a postcode may be insufficient—so some people might include an extra address line or extend these lines to 30 characters each.

The telephone field allows for most international telephone numbers. We are suggesting a character field to allow the numbers to be broken up with spaces or hyphens (e.g. 01 123 4567 or 01-123-4567) as an aid to legibility. (A numeric field would allow only 011234567.)

Size: 187 × 200 = 37400 bytes. Say 75 K to allow file to grow; say 150 K if sequential updates are to be carried out.

Q 10.10 (*a*) key field (customer account code) plus data depending on type of transaction, for example:

- *For an invoice:* Invoice number, date, amount(s)—net, VAT, freight, total etc.
- *For a payment:* Date received, amount, cheque number, related invoice number.

Some field in the record must show what it represents, e.g. invoice or payment.

(*b*) key field (name plus initials or student number), plus transaction data, for example:

- *To update,* say, examination results (subjects, dates of exam, grades)
- *To add* new students, personal details (address, telephone, names of parents or guardians, date of birth, sex, subjects etc.)
- *To delete* a student, only the key is needed.

An extra field would be needed in this example to show which type of transaction each record carried (update, addition or deletion).

(*c*) key field (usually part number or stock number), plus transaction data, e.g. number issued or received, description (if a new or changed item), bin location (i.e. where to find the item), price information, re-order quantities, re-order levels etc. As with the other examples, a transaction code would be needed *within* the record, so that the update program could tell whether to insert, delete or change master file records.

? **Q 10.11 and Q 10.12** The transactions file is requiring amendments to records 00120 (amend the main location field to California, USA) and 00140 (amend the minimum population field to 20).

Record 00150 is to be deleted (so no transaction details are necessary—the record is to be erased completely) and Record 00020 is to be amended (maximum population to be 180).

This much should be obvious so long as the students understand the significance of the transaction codes A, D (and I, not included here).

However, the updating may be incomplete if the file is sequential and only sequential access is possible. The problem arises because record 00020 is out of sequence in the transactions file. For this update to run successfully in a sequential system, the transactions file would need initial sorting so that record 00020 was at the beginning, where it belongs. (The other records are in order.)

Of course, this problem would not arise if indexed or direct access is possible.

? **Q 10.13** Sorting transactions is pointless if indexed access to the master is used. In this case the master file has no logical beginning or end.

? **Q 10.14** In both cases, the program would fail *unless* the programmer had taken precautions. Depending on the sophistication of the operating software, the files could be seriously corrupted by such a mistake. The files would have to be meticulously checked, and restored if necessary. Any update program should be designed to cater for these errors, report them and continue processing subsequent records without damage to the files.

? **Q 10.15** Yes, because the key fields are numbered in tens. The record keys, 0010 and 0011, leave no room for record insertion, unless the whole numbering system were changed. If there is the slightest chance of needing to insert in this way, gaps should be left between the key values.

BASIC programs are stored as sequential files. Students may have written BASIC programs which, on debugging, required insertion of new lines. If the gaps between line numbers are too small, the whole program may need renumbering. Discuss how a BASIC interpreter allows record amendments, insertions and deletions.

? **Q 10.16** Frequently used files are ideally kept on-line, generally on disk. The same applies when updates are frequent: it is tiresome, for instance, to load and unload media (especially tapes) too often. If the update is regular however, say every evening, tape or disk may be equally convenient.

If the data is needed for immediate enquiry, tape is virtually ruled out. Magnetic or, increasingly, optical disk would allow the necessary speed of response.

Q 10.17 This question can only be answered by practical experience. If at all possible, students should be given the opportunity to use any available database software. Such software is not always easy to get to grips with and a familiarisation time will be needed to gain a fair impression of its power and speed.

To give students a point of comparison it is worth dividing the class into small teams, half of which build and manipulate a data structure with the help of a DBMS while the other half carry out the *same* exercise using an ordinary programming language and files. The teams using DBMSs should take significantly less time or achieve greater sophistication in their projects than their colleagues.

There is interminable debate in the computer industry as to what constitutes a *true* database or DBMS, and which DBMSs are *truly* relational! Teachers can happily ignore this, but should beware of some 'file handling' systems (claiming to be DBMSs, and sold in the education sector) which do not facilitate relating, or linking, individual data elements. There need *not* be any physical, permanent link established, as long as data can be readily related (as in Fig. 10.10 of the students' text, for instance) the system is likely to be useful. It may also be called a DBMS.

11 Reliability and Security

Students often display an extraordinary (and unfounded) faith in the 'intelligence' of computer systems. They may expect the computer to reject anything which is clearly nonsense (such as a bill for −£1 000 000 or £FRED, or a cheque for £0.00) without realising that a computer rejects nothing *unless it is told to* (explicitly or implicitly). You may need to stress that computer systems have no common sense at all, but they blindly obey the rules we give them. This may change, but it has not yet.

Similarly there is a tendency to regard the reliability of systems as absolute. For instance few people, young or old, *really* see the need for back-up copies, until they have lost their only copy of a file which took hours to create.

DISCUSSION POINTS

? **Q 11.1** We cannot be certain who to blame for the letter about the £0.00 debt. Perhaps a directive from senior management to 'prosecute all debtors' was taken too literally. The result could have been a program specification stating, say, 'letter 3 (threat of court action) must be printed for all customers owing money'.

But that mistake could have triggered a threat for a 1p debt; what about 0p? Perhaps it was a rounding error; the lady *might* have owed a tiny fraction of a penny (the result of some charging formula) which was rounded down to £0.00 when printed out but may have been still *stored* as a fraction, which the 'threatening letter' program took to be a debt.

Suggested safeguards:
The systems analyst should have clarified the requirement with management, agreeing clear rules for the issue of such letters (e.g. including a limit of £50).

The system cannot have been *tested* with enough realistic data; if it had been, examination of the output should have highlighted the problem.

In any event, surely there should be an administrative check on such a serious letter. Unless the organisation was threatening thousands of people daily (which would suggest a grave problem with their *modus operandi*) a manual check would be advisable.

In the anchor case, it was simply too easy for the clerk to spend large sums of money, just by keying in a four-digit number. The system probably provided little or no checking on (*a*) the clerk's authority to enter a major purchase, or (*b*) whether the part number entered corresponded to the item actually required.

Suggested safeguards:
There should be some cash limit on an individual clerk's ordering authority, which the ordering system should check.

There should be *at least* a description of the part displayed on screen for the operator to confirm. But a tired or bored clerk might just hit 'enter' without *reading* the description; better to make the operator *key in* a description, which the system would attempt to match with the stored version.

As will be seen later in Q 11.4, a check digit on a part number would prevent a simple keying error.

Someone should, of course, have checked the destination when the anchor was actually dispatched.

? **Q 11.2** The hash total of account numbers is 29836. This number has no real meaning *per se*, but the system could (as with the money total) ask the operator to input this hash total, manually calculated, for comparison with the computed total. Such totals could also be used, say, when the monthly analysis is carried out, to ensure that all batches of data have been processed.

? **Q 11.3** (b) is wrong; (a), (c) and (d) are correct.

Why does it work?
Let the original number be $11x + R$.

Expanding the number by an extra digit, by writing R units on the end gives a new value

$$10\,(11x + R) + R = 110x + 11R$$

and the factor of 11 is guaranteed. Good students ought to be able to prove this by themselves.

? **Q 11.4** *Some* modulo 11 checks *will* be fooled by swopping digits.

? **Q 11.5** (b) and (c) are wrong; (a) and (d) are correct.

Since each digit in the original number is multiplied by a different weighting and none of the numbers involved can have factors in common with 11, then transposing two digits is bound to upset the check calculation.

But why 11?
Inevitably, you will be asked 'But why 11?' You can best answer this by showing that a similar method using a lower modulo is *not* foolproof.

Example: A weighted modulo 4 check on the number given in the main text does not work (because the transposed digits and corresponding weights have factors in common with 4).

Calculate the check digit for the correct account number 47856.

$4 \times 6 = 24$
$7 \times 5 = 35$
$8 \times 4 = 32$
$5 \times 3 = 15$
$6 \times 2 = 12$

118

This much is identical to the original calculation in the pupil text.

We need a check digit 2 as $120 \equiv 0$ (modulo 4).

With check digit, the account number is written 4 7 8 5 6 2 and the correctly written number checks as follows:

$4 \times 6 = 24$
$7 \times 5 = 35$
$8 \times 4 = 32$
$5 \times 3 = 15$
$6 \times 2 = 12$
$2 \times 1 = 2$

120 $\equiv 0$ (modulo 4)

Now suppose the 6 and the 8 are transposed, as in the main text:

These interchanged

$4 \times 6 =$	24
$7 \times 5 =$	35
$6 \times 4 =$	24
$5 \times 3 =$	15
$8 \times 2 =$	16
$2 \times 1 =$	2
	116 $\equiv 0$ (modulo 4)

Using a modulo 4 system, this *incorrect* number is apparently valid!

For very long codes modulo 11 might *still* fail if a weighting factor of 11 is ever used.

? **Q 11.6** (*a*) The weighted modulo 11 check digit is 7.

(*b*) ISBNs also use weighted modulo 11.

Some students might like to design and code a program which generates a modulo 11 check digit upon input of a number up to 9 digits long.

? **Q 11.7** The characters are: 'BYE!

The parity bit for the Y should be 0.

? **Q 11.8** (*a*) Cashtill system:

Require customer to key in a personal identification number (which is *not* printed on the card).

Retain card after three unsuccessful attempts to key in this number (in case card has been stolen).

Alarm automatically triggered by any attempt at physical tampering. All cards should have a withdrawal limit.

(*b*) Student records system:

Prevent unauthorised access by careful password control and/or restriction on terminal/micro usage.

Meticulous verification and checking on data entry to prevent inaccurate data getting into the system.

(*c*) Company's weekly wages system:

Same as (*b*) plus separate responsibilities if possible e.g. have data entry, processing, distribution of payslips all done by different people. Minimise cash handling by giros, direct funds transfer (rather than cash in pay packets).

Many companies already use external computer bureaux to run their payroll systems, not just for convenience but also to enhance their payroll confidentiality.

Q 11.9 The obvious risk is losing hours of work, and so all material relating to the program should be secure.

Name, date, number and file all paperwork (specifications, algorithms, flowcharts, listings, test data and results) carefully. When a large program has been keyed in and stored on, say, floppy disk, it is prudent to take a back-up copy and keep it in a separate place from the original. Take careful note of the time and date of back-ups: each time the program is amended, a new back-up copy should be taken.

A simple form (see Fig. 11.1) will help to keep track of back-ups.

COMPUTER STUDIES—BACK-UP LOG SHEET

Back-up date	time	Programmer's name and initials	File/program name and size		Back-up disk number
7/3/90	4.15p.m.	BLOGGS J.	ECON ØØ2	12K	B ØØ1

Fig. 11.1 Suggested back-up log sheet

Part D Computers in Action

12 Case Study: URD Ltd

Some effort has been made to avoid both business and accounting jargon in this chapter. 'Debit' and 'credit' appear only on Fig. 12.2 in the pupil's book, which shows the layout of a manual ledger account. Similarly, reference has been avoided to 'posting' transactions ('entering' or 'inputting' has been used). Bear in mind, however, that any packaged sales ledger software to which you may have access may well use accounting terms, and so it is as well to check it thoroughly first before using it in class.

It is suggested that you discuss some basic *business* issues with your students before they read this case study. What are the objectives of a business? What are the major problems it may face? Without wishing to turn the course into one on business studies, this will be time well spent. It is impossible to understand the real benefits of any system without some idea about the problems that the system is trying to solve.

DISCUSSION POINTS

? **Q 12.1** Many growing businesses face this type of cash crisis, caused by too much rather than too little business. URD Ltd. is having to pay out large sums for stock *several months before* it receives payment for sales. The faster the company's growth, the worse this problem becomes.

We should be cautious about recommending *anything* at this stage, let alone a computer system. Stress how important it is to discover much more about the current problems before coming up with solutions.

? **Q 12.2** After individual attempts, 'brainstorm' solutions to this question. Wages, salaries and stock or materials are of course the biggest expenditure items for many companies. Remember overheads (rent, rates, heat, light, telephone etc.), administration (stationery, printing, copying etc.), capital costs (machinery, premises etc.) selling costs (cars, fuel, expenses, commissions, advertising, exhibitions etc.), research and development (these are heavy for, say, drug companies), professional costs (lawyers, accountants etc.). Sales are usually the only source of income, but there might be royalties, interest, capital gains etc.

? **Q 12.3** Probable reasons:

(*a*) So that two operators could simultaneously access the system (there may be too much volume for one machine to handle). It may also be possible to keep operation going with only one microcomputer, perhaps even using floppy disks, and so there is a security benefit, too.

(*b*) So that common files (customer master and open-item files) can be used by both machines. The software must prevent simultaneous attempts to update the same record (this safeguard is called 'record locking').

(*c*) Again, for security; processing could continue if one printer broke down. Perhaps one printer was a high-speed machine for internal reports, while the other produced letter quality output for presentation purposes.

? **Q 12.4** Do not underestimate the time it takes to set up a demonstration system; you need a reasonable volume of data to make it realistic. Allow students to try various functions without too much prompting, in order to gauge the ease of use.

? **Q 12.5** (*a*) Whenever goods (or services) are sold.

(*b*) When goods are returned, when orders are cancelled for which an invoice has already been issued, possibly when a customer pays too much or (rarely) when a discount is granted after invoicing.

? **Q 12.6** Adjustment transactions are the only way of correcting errors; e.g. invoices/credits/cash entered for the wrong amount, or against the wrong customer etc. Note that packages may refer to adjustments as 'transfers' or 'debit memos' and 'credit memos'.

? **Q 12.7** Any outstanding invoice would be cleared, and the *excess* cash would remain on the open-item file as an unallocated cash balance.

FURTHER CASE STUDY WORK

The newsagents and Post Office exercises at the end of the chapter will lend themselves to extended case studies. At the very least students should be encouraged to design the appropriate files/record structures along with algorithms for data entry, update or retrieval.

Having gone that far, it is worthwhile and rewarding to create the actual systems. Team work is a good method for these assignments, provided that no individual hogs all the design or all the coding etc.

Modest systems can be developed and tested more quickly with the help of a database package. Some people may prefer to work from scratch and use only a programming language such as BASIC. As in previous cases, it is particularly valuable if students have a chance to compare the speed and effectiveness of the two approaches.

Other suggestions for creation and manipulation of data structures:

(*a*) Football (or other sport) league tables. This could allow input of results, calculation of points, goal differences, etc. and automatic rearrangement of the tables.

(*b*) Estate agents' particulars of houses, flats etc. This application can provide an interesting database structure. It can even be developed into role plays, where *buyers* approach *agents* with specific needs (e.g. two bedrooms, garage, quiet location, price range etc.). A well designed and executed system will allow rapid search of the database to reveal possible properties. Can anyone develop a system so friendly that the *buyer* can interrogate it without assistance or prompting?

Individuals should be encouraged to come up with their own ideas; applications related to their own interests are extremely motivating.

13 Case Study: Office Computing

DISCUSSION POINTS

? **Q 13.1** *Advantages:* All staff work with the same system; this saves space and duplication of effort; the company has a more complete picture of its customers.

Disadvantages: Some people are 'possessive' of information and may resist using a new, centralised system; there could be conflict if two people want a particular record; inaccurate information could damage the whole company and so someone must be entrusted with keeping the file(s) accurate and current.

? **Q 13.2** (*a*) Students will need prompting to attempt commonsense estimates of field lengths. It is sensible to be over generous with file sizes, to allow for growth and editing of files.

Say:	Customer number	6 characters	6
	Name, address and telephone number	6 fields × 25 characters	150
	Languages	3 fields × 10 characters	30
	Enquiries	20 × (date 6, code 4, response 25)	700
	Courses	50 × (code 4, fee 5, date 6, locations 5)	1000
	Contacts	5 × (name 25, position 15, extension 5)	225
	Total		2111

Thus each customer needs about 2.1 K of file space.

(*b*) For the whole file, therefore, 2.1 K × 200 (customers) = 420 K bytes. (slight overestimate as 1 K = 1024 bytes.)
1 megabyte would not be excessive to allow for growth and editing.

? **Q 13.3** Information that *could* be included: course title, course code, duration, timetable, language, course fees, minimum and maximum class sizes, whether courses are residential, prerequisites, possible lecturers, scheduled dates and locations, bookings, places available.

Encourage students to produce a record layout along the lines of Fig. 13.1 and to estimate record size.

? **Q 13.4** Dealers will often agree over the telephone to send brief details of packages available. But do not direct the whole class to one dealer. Magazines can be helpful too; they often review database and other packages. This exercise might encourage some pupils to visit the local library, which will have a computer section and possibly some magazines.

? **Q 13.5** (*a*) *Accident:* If anything, it will be less secure (owing to the elimination of duplication and the sensitivity of magnetic media) unless precautions are taken. Back-up copies need to be made of all files as a matter of course (one reason for dual disk systems). Occasional printed listings are sensible, too.

(*b*) *Theft:* Centralisation can assist security, but one floppy disk is much easier to steal than 200 paper files. Security measures such as passwords may help to prevent illicit access, but a disgruntled employee could pass them on (see Chapter 11).

? **Q 13.6** A typewriter cannot *store* information (although some electronic typewriters now do store a little). Thus correction is difficult and messy (using fluids etc.). Words, sentences and paragraphs cannot be moved to another place in the text. 'Top copies' of a document can be made only by retyping. (Carbon copies and photocopies are often unacceptable, e.g. when dealing with customers.)

Word processors overcome all these limitations, and can automatically centre or justify text, print page numbers etc. More advanced functions including searching and replacing, underlining, bold type, and even switching to italic and other typefaces if these are possible on the printer being used.

? **Q 13.9** Assuming that all the MEPs with their addresses were stored on the Eurotraining system, the steps might be:

1 Use the database software to extract four files, one for each native tongue.

2 Set up each of the four letters for merging, with codes to indicate where individual names and addresses are to be inserted (Note differences in address layouts, e.g. French addresses have postcodes in a different place). See Fig. 13.5.

3 Merge each of these letters with the appropriate address file.

4 Check and sign the letters.

5 Put in envelopes and post.

Checking is vital for any letter, especially so for mailshots like this. In one case we have encountered, the merging process went haywire and letters were produced saying not 'Dear Mr Jenkins' as intended, but 'Dear 0344 45622'!

? **Q 13.11** This can obviously be a rapid process, enabling a large number of 'personal' letters to be sent to different people in a short space of time. If they were general enquiries it might be an excellent method, far more likely to obtain a positive response than a 'Dear Sir/Madam' letter.

But if, as in Fig. 13.7, the letter is an application for a job, the applicant would be better advised to write individual letters in which the applicant's skills or qualifications can be related to each particular vacancy.

? **Q 13.12** Additions to basic pay might include overtime, bonuses (paid for various reasons, e.g. productivity, good timekeeping etc.), commission (paid to salespeople and others who sell products or services for the company), loans (e.g. for season tickets), refunds (due to previous excessive deductions), backdated pay increases and profit shares.

? **Q 13.13** (*a*) Hourly rate of pay would have to be stored. The overtime pay rates would also be needed, or possibly the ratios (1.5 and 2.0) to enable the computer to calculate overtime rates.

(*b*) Hours worked at normal rate, overtime hours at time-and-a-half and at double time, would have to be separately recorded (e.g. on clock cards) and input each week for each employee.

? **Q 13.14** Programs are needed to carry out the following:

(*a*) Set up the employee master file and parameter file.

(*b*) Amend employee details (corrections, pay rise, address change etc.).

(*c*) Add employee records when a new person is hired.

(*d*) Delete employee records when someone leaves.

Note: Strictly the employee record would be marked as a leaver and not actually deleted until after the tax year had ended.

(*e*) Amend parameters (e.g. changes to tax/NI/sick pay rates/bands as the result of a Budget).

(*f*) Print details for bank credits and transfers or cheques.

(*g*) Produce reports for management on payroll costs.

(*h*) Produce reports required by auditors, and by the Government (especially at year end).

(*i*) Display a 'menu' that enables the operator rapidly to select and run the required program.

Typically there would be separate programs for each of the above functions, although some systems may combine functions into larger programs.

14 Case Study: The Electronic Office

DISCUSSION POINTS

? **Q 14.1** See Chapter 6.

? **Q 14.2** Floppy disks (floppies) are sometimes retained for back-up purposes, but even using very high-density floppies, several are needed to back up all the files on one hard disk. In this case the company backs up its data using high-speed tape drives.

A single floppy disk drive is still useful with a hard disk system, however, for *loading new software;* most packaged programs are supplied on floppies. Usually the program would be installed by copying to hard disk before running it, but some software suppliers still use a method of copy protection (to stop illegal copying) which requires the master floppy disk to be placed in the disk drive every time the program is to be run.

Floppy disks are also useful for occasional *transfers of data* between machines which are *not* linked via any network.

? **Q 14.3** See Chapter 8.

? **Q 14.4** For a company to gain the maximum benefit from electronic mail, all its locations should have the facilities. Communication *between* sites is at least as useful as communication within a single site.

The spread of electronic mail has been fairly slow because of the 'critical mass' problem; until most organisations use it, its usefulness will be limited.

It may be worth noting that, when *telephones* were in their infancy, a senior Post Office official proclaimed that no one could possibly want one. His reasoning was that even if you were foolish enough to wish to use a telephone, it would be impossible because nobody else would have one.

? **Q 14.5** The electronic mail (email) market is now developing rapidly. Systems such as British Telecom Gold offer a wide range of facilities, such as telex, bulletin board, telemessages, radiopaging and on-line databases.

Current information can be obtained from the suppliers and magazines such as *Telelink* (published by Database Publications) and *Communications Management* (EMAP Business and Computer Publications).

Users access their electronic mailbox by keying in a unique 'identity' (sometimes called 'user-ID') and an individually-chosen password. Both of these should be kept secret; they should never be 'lent' to friends or colleagues.

? **Q 14.6** *All* the available pages on a teletext service must be transmitted in sequence, because it is a one-way system. Therefore, if the page you select has just been broadcast, you must wait until it 'comes round again'. This is a key reason why teletext services are limited to a few hundred pages; if even one thousand pages were transmitted, the delay would be unacceptable.

? **Q 14.7** The user input goes only as far as the decoding electronics attached to the special teletext TV set. This stores the user's requested page number and matches it with the incoming page numbers, displaying data when the match succeeds.

? **Q 14.8** A viewdata system transmits only *selected* information to the user; this means that thousands, even millions of pages can be provided. (The user can even go beyond a single host computer to access others, e.g. via the Gateway software on Prestel.)

Two-way communication permits facilities such as teleshopping (including booking travel, holidays etc.), home banking, bulletin boards, telesoftware, sophisticated database searches as well as forms of electronic mail.

? **Q 14.9** The longer any password is used, the more likely it is to fall into the wrong hands. People may get careless and write their passwords down, give them to colleagues, or even be *observed* keying them in (screen display should always be suppressed when passwords are entered).

Users of some viewdata services employ automatic logging-on techniques (to save repeatedly keying in a fiddly sequence of characters). If the codes for automatic logon are stored on-line, they could be read remotely; many on-line services routinely 'enquire' as to a terminal's identity. This can result in revelation of passwords. Frequent changes afford a simple but effective safeguard.

? **Q 14.10** Even a very fast typist, capable of, say, 80 words per minute, is keying at $(80 \times 5)/60 = 6.66$ characters per second, a baud rate of 66.66. When modems can often transmit at 1200 baud, it makes sense to compose electronic messages off-line, and then transmit them at high speed, thus minimising charges for 'connect time'.

? **Q 14.11** Examples might include:

- Textbooks—could this one be more up to date if delivered electronically?
- TV and radio—video and tape recorders already allow 'time-shifting' of viewing and listening.
- Newspapers, magazines and comics—would electronic format permit a more 'personalised' publication, omitting, say, fashion pages or football reports according to preference?
- Train and bus timetables—printed ones have to be frequently replaced.
- Top 40 music charts—would there be any point in updating them in real time?

15 Shops

DISCUSSION POINTS

? **Q 15.1** Some everyday stock problems illustrate stock-control better than others. Petrol is usually replaced on an *ad hoc* basis (but in response to an automated warning system—the red line on the petrol gauge indicates the 're-order level'). Good grocery examples are items like butter and sugar which are used for various purposes. Baking a large birthday cake will cause unusual demand.

? **Q 15.2** Warehouse space is an expensive commodity. Many goods are perishable and simply do not have a shelf life of two months. The over-high level of stocks would tie up money that could be put to better use.

? **Q 15.3** Other information: shelf life; order quantities; prices; possible discounts; delivery times; special promotions; alternative suppliers; advertising campaigns and other promotions; importance of stock item (e.g. milk is more vital than, say, Brazil nuts).

? **Q 15.4** (x) standard order quantity (fixed by shopkeeper, but must not be less than (ix)).

? **Q 15.5** Demand; delivery time; storage space.

'Demand', of course, begs many questions. Demand for some items (e.g. cranberry sauce) is seasonal; others (e.g. ice-cream) depend upon the weather; while still others (e.g. confectionery) are affected by special promotions and competitions.

Larger businesses perform statistical analyses on historical sales data in order to determine trends and probabilities of different demand levels. Exploring this area may confuse some students.

? **Q 15.6** No order would be printed in this example as four cases are already on order (data item (viii)).

? **Q 15.7** The shopkeeper must update the file when an order is delivered, so (viii) reverts to 0 (in addition to storing cases and replenishing shelves).

? **Q 15.8** The stock master file must be indexed so that data held on particular items (identifiable by EAN or description) is easy to check. Without an index the whole file might have to be read in order to access a single item.

? **Q 15.9** *Number in stock* only. The others are already on file and the computer will use these to prompt the shopkeeper.

? **Q 15.10** Two additional files would normally be sufficient: one for suppliers' names and addresses and one for orders. Possible record formats could be;

Orders file:

Supplier number	Order number	Order date	Delivery date	Invoice number	Invoice date	Gross amt £	Net amt £	VAT £	Date paid

Suppliers' file:

Supplier number	Supplier name	Address line 1	Address line 2	Address line 3	Telephone	Terms (e.g. 30 days)	Payment method (cash/cheque)

The various items included on one order would probably not be stored individually as the shopkeeper can check his order copy as needed. *Unpaid bills* (explain that 'bill' and 'invoice' are synonymous) are orders with *delivery date* entered but with *date paid* left blank. Similarly, the computer would extract *outstanding orders* by seeking blank *delivery dates*. Total *VAT payments* can be calculated by totalling *VAT £* for the appropriate range of *date paid*.

Note that further programs are needed to enter invoices, deliveries etc. as well as to update suppliers' names and addresses. Writing and testing these programs would take many months and so obviously a package is preferable.

? **Q 15.11** *The customer* should find the new system beneficial in most respects: itemised bills are easy to check and fewer errors and faster checkouts are obviously welcome. Faster turnover in the shop may mean keener prices. However, the likely drift to prepacked goods rather than fresh items and the ease with which the shop may alter prices are disadvantages.

The management, once the initial investment has been made, should be happy with most aspects of the system and be able to offer a better but cheaper service to the customer.

The shop staff will possibly suffer some job losses and those kept on will have to learn new (but simple) procedures.

? **Q 15.12** Automated POS terminals do not altogether eliminate the need for occasional stocktakes. 'Shrinkage' i.e. loss of stock to dishonest staff and shop-lifters and 'returns' will bypass the POS procedures and must be accounted for.

The warehouseman will not need to write down descriptions of the items he is counting. He will use the light pen to read the bar code on the shelf (or on the packages themselves), count the number in stock and punch that number into his portable processor.

? **Q 15.13** If the system 'goes down' it would be sensible to close the shop to new customers; there will be more than enough to do if disruption to the computer records (from the customers already in the store) is to be avoided.

The checkout staff will have to record the items taken from the store by these customers either by recording the product numbers (although this is likely to be inaccurate given the ease with which digits could be transposed) or by noting down the item *description*, and the quantity the customer is buying. Price details would also be included on the receipt so that the checkout staff can work out the total (they no longer have the computer to work it out for them). In effect, staff would be writing traditional receipts:

2 × 450g Heinz Beans @ 32p	=	64p
1 large Kelloggs Branflakes @ 88p	=	88p
Total	=	£1.52

This would be slow and customers would be unhappy.

? **Q 15.14** The Kimball tag *must* carry an item code and generally includes a (printed) price for the customer's convenience. There is no need for the tag to encode shop details or for the computer to code the price since these can be easily input to the computer in other ways.

? **Q 15.15** At least: store identification code number; item codes; sales for the day and, possibly, closing stock.

? **Q 15.16** If the same warehouse is to supply a number of different shops, then the delivery schedules need to be carefully planned. A variety of factors must be taken into account: the loads the vans can carry, the distance between the shops, likely travel times and fuel costs.

On the one hand, the lorry drivers must all work as full a day as possible but not incur an unacceptable number of hours overtime on the other.

The calculations, although seemingly simple enough in principle, are in fact quite complicated in detail. It is natural for the supermarket chains to pass the job over to the computer.

EXERCISES 15

Q 5 (i) A simple order form could be as shown below. In practice, the toothpaste is probably *not* sold in tubes but in packages of tens.

Order Number | P | T | P | | | | | |

Date | | | | | | |

To: Pearly Toothpaste Company
35 Wisdom Street
CAVITY MO 1AR

Please deliver to:
Shoes the Chemist,
Pharmacopoeia
Drugsville.

Brand	Quantity (tubes)
TPA	
TPB	
TPC	
TPD	
TPE	
Total	

(ii) A possible flowchart is shown on the opposite page. Alternative solutions are possible. Our 'Brandcount' takes values from 1 to 5 as there are five inputs; five input lines also work but are less flexible.

(iii) Although all the relevant information may fit on a punched card, it would not be sensible for the chemist to use them: a card punch and reader system would cost more than his microcomputer which in any case has a keyboard.

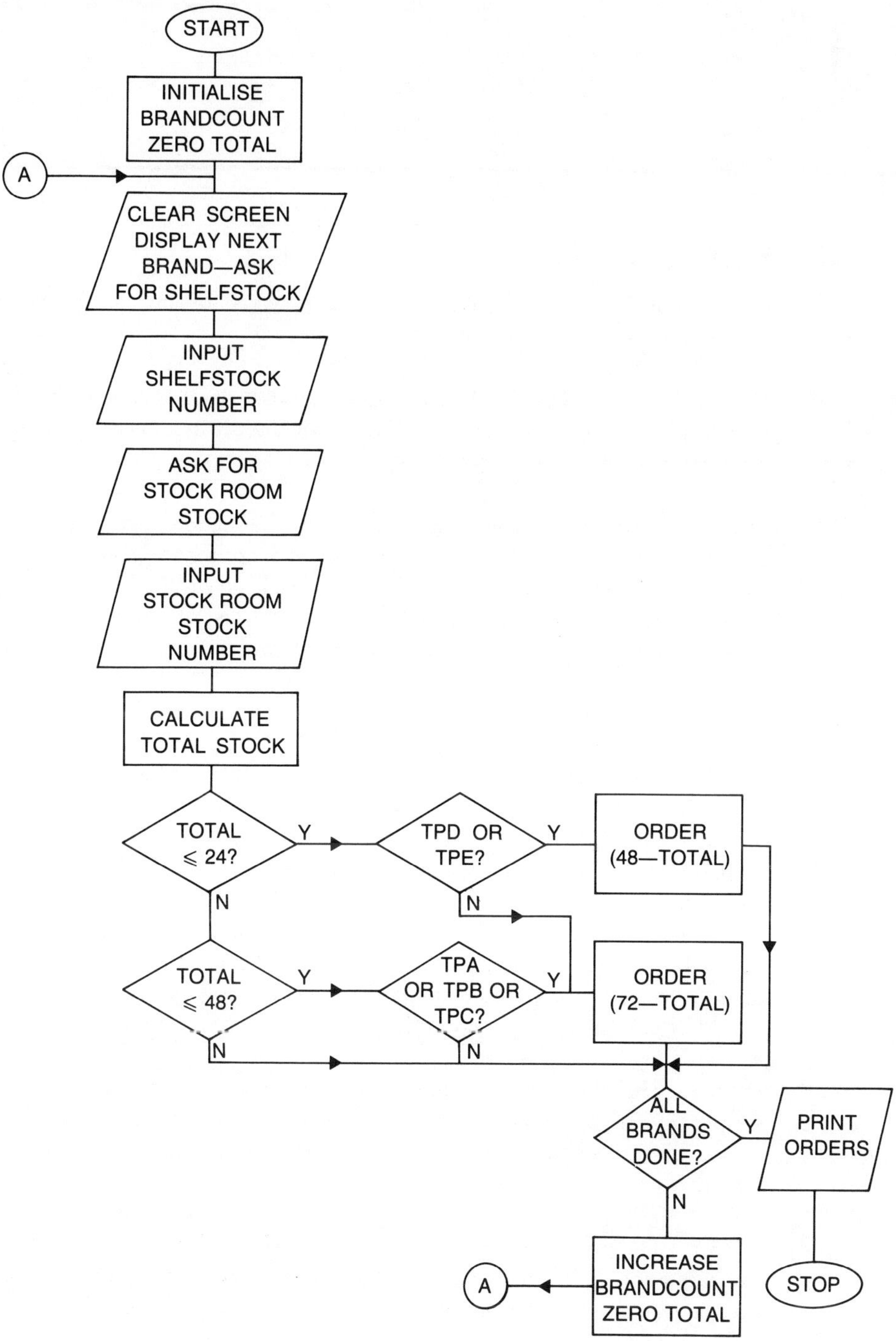
START
INITIALISE BRANDCOUNT ZERO TOTAL
A
CLEAR SCREEN DISPLAY NEXT BRAND—ASK FOR SHELFSTOCK
INPUT SHELFSTOCK NUMBER
ASK FOR STOCK ROOM STOCK
INPUT STOCK ROOM STOCK NUMBER
CALCULATE TOTAL STOCK
TOTAL ⩽ 24?
Y
N
TPD OR TPE?
Y
N
ORDER (48—TOTAL)
TOTAL ⩽ 48?
Y
N
TPA OR TPB OR TPC?
Y
N
ORDER (72—TOTAL)
ALL BRANDS DONE?
Y
N
PRINT ORDERS
STOP
INCREASE BRANDCOUNT ZERO TOTAL
A

16 Libraries

DISCUSSION POINTS

? **Q 16.1** By losing touch with known borrowers; by borrowers returning books to another library; by misfiling.

? **Q 16.2** A large library is likely to issue thousands of books in one day; it must organise a day's file sensibly. Usually tickets are arranged alphabetically by author or by the library's book number.

? **Q 16.3** If the library moves the ticket from the file relevant to the last date stamp it is then at the mercy of the borrower who may or may not pencil in the correct return date; inevitably, some tickets would be lost. Instead, libraries leave the ticket in the file relevant to the last official date stamp and insert a note to the effect 'renewed by telephone; return due 29th May'.

? **Q 16.4** A library can simply and effectively restrict members to, say, five books by only issuing five tickets. This may seem trivial, but contrasts with a computerised system in which it is a lot more troublesome to stop readers borrowing excessive numbers of books.

? **Q 16.5** If the library tickets were scattered throughout the filing system it would be *possible*, but a very lengthy and tedious business to find the tickets belonging to an individual. (Checking *book* details written at the very top of the book-cards is easier.) The library could not itemise past loans; any attempt to write down books taken out over a period by selected individuals would be extremely slow (again this is in contrast to a computerised system).

? **Q 16.6** The library could find out how often a book had been borrowed simply by looking at the date stamp. To do this systematically for every book in the library stock is another *possible* but time-consuming and tedious activity.

? **Q 16.7** The postcard needs to show the readers address and details of the overdue book. It follows that the library must have an up-to-date address on the reader's ticket and the author and title on the book-card.

A friendly approach to your local library might well elicit a specimen copy of the postcard that it actually uses.

NEWSHIRE COUNTY LIBRARIES
Barchester Branch.
Date: as postmark

May I remind you that the following book(s) were due for return on ....

Author	Title
....	....
....	....
....	....
....	....

There is now a postage charge to pay as well as a fine.

Theo Bosse, County Librarian

PLEASE BRING THIS CARD WITH YOU WHEN YOU RETURN THE BOOKS TO THE LIBRARY

Fig. 16.1 Library reminder postcard requesting the return of an overdue book

When the postcard is sent, a note to the effect 'first reminder sent 2/6/87: postage cost 13p' should be placed in the ticket. The library needs to know that the reader has been reminded and how many times lest the matter is later disputed.

? **Q 16.8** The library would probably keep a 'blacklist' of banned readers. But a reader might still manage to use his tickets successfully if the librarian does not recognise him or the name and does not check the blacklist.

? **Q 16.9** The Dewey Decimal System, named after its American inventor Melvil Dewey, is an international system by which books are divided into subjects, each subject into 10 sub-categories, each of these into 100 sub-divisions, each division into another 10 or 100 categories and so on. The system is continually revised (by the US Library of Congress) and reached its twentieth edition in 1986.

Such a system may not be of much use to a highly specialised library. A category such as 'medicine' might not be of much help to the library of the Royal College of Surgeons.

? **Q 16.10** A new book requires the allocation of a Dewey Decimal Number (to be marked on its spine); and the allocation of a library book number (the library probably does not depend on ISBNs as these do not cater for duplicate copies of a single title). An index card must be prepared for the book; the library's possession stamp must be marked inside the book and the library's label (which usually doubles up as a date-stamp sticker and book-card holder) must be stuck inside; a book-card must be prepared showing the classification number, author and title; paperbacks also need stiff covers.

? **Q 16.11** To establish that the book is on loan, the librarian must comb through all the cards in the returns files (these are called 'issues trays' in librarians' jargon; we have deliberately used a term that stresses their rôle in the filing process). This is time-consuming and there is a good chance that the card would be missed. Assuming the book-card is found then it must be marked in some way (perhaps a red card is inserted inside the ticket) to indicate that the book must not go back onto the shelves when it is returned but be kept back so that the customer's request may be met.

? **Q 16.12** Once the requested book materialises (whether or not through another library) the librarian must inform the reader of its arrival. It follows that the request form should double as the postcard that the librarian sends. The reader is, after all, the best person to fill in his own address even if the librarian wishes to check the book details. Again, the local library would probably let you have a specimen postcard.

NEWSHIRE COUNTY LIBRARIES
Barchester Branch.
Date: as postmark.

Your recent request

☐ is ready for your collection

☐ is unobtainable

Author ....
(Block letters please)

Title (or subject) ....

....

Catalogue Number ☐☐☐☐☐☐☐☐☐☐☐☐☐☐

Publisher .... Price ....

Source of information ....

Latest date of use ....

1. Shall we borrow outside Newshire? YES/NO
2. Is a substitute acceptable? YES/NO
3. Is a photocopy acceptable? YES/NO

PLEASE BRING THIS CARD WITH YOU

Please fill in your name and address

Fig. 16.2 Notification to borrower of the arrival in the library of a requested book

? **Q 16.13** The validation program would ensure the catalogue number was of acceptable form. It might also check each word of the title against a 'dictionary' and the author's initials and surname as alphabetic.

? **Q 16.14** The transactions file is sorted into catalogue number (assuming this is the key field) so that the amendments to the (sequential) master file can be made on one search of the tape.

? **Q 16.15** The transactions file and old master file are retained (as the new 'father' file) in case of loss of the new master file.

? **Q 16.17** The book-stock master file would have a layout something like this.

Book Number (or ISBN)	Author Surname	Author Initials	Title	Subject Classifn.	Copy Number	Total Number Copies Held	Library Holding This Copy	Number of Times Borrowed	Publisher	Cost
(15)	(20)	(5)	(100)	(15)	(3)	(3)	(20)	(4)	(20)	(5)

Fig. 16.3 Book-stock master file layout

Estimated field lengths are shown in brackets. The total is 210 bytes. The book (catalogue) number would be the key field *not* the author (because of duplication).

? **Q 16.18** Membership tickets must be durable enough to withstand public handling without the bar-coded details being obscured.

? **Q 16.19** Since the system centres on the computer at the library headquarters, there is no need to restrict members to one particular library; the ticket is valid at any computerised library in that county (Newshire).

? **Q 16.20** The librarian must check that the book is not overdue and charge a fine if it is. Otherwise the books that are returned can be checked into the computer system at *any* time that day, as the returns will not be processed until the cassette tape or floppy disk is delivered to the computer centre, and there is no ticket to hand back to the reader as in the manual system.

? **Q 16.21** There is unlikely to be sufficient memory space in the microcomputer to make signalling of overdue books possible. (Too many people are late with their books.) However, in an on-line system, the *loans file* could be directly interrogated and so it *would* be possible to set an 'overdue' trap at the check-in counter.

? **Q 16.22** and **Q 16.23** As the hardware is not expensive, the library could have third and fourth light pens and tape on standby. In a small urban borough, the library headquarters could have one or two on standby for the whole service and deliver them immediately a library telephones to report a failure.

Some county services continue to keep book-cards inside the books, and so in the event of failure, the librarians would need only to note down the name of the borrower who takes a book out and keep it with the appropriate cards. Unfortunately, if the library does not remove the cards whenever the book is issued, as in the manual system, readers tend to use them as bookmarks and then lose them altogether.

If a back-up card system is not used, then librarians will have to write down details of each loan by hand. A prudent librarian would *not* try to 'get away' with just writing down book and readers numbers; without immediate computerised verification enough of the numbers are likely to be misrecorded to upset the entire system.

If a computerised system develops a reputation for unreliability the county library service could have real problems; human nature is, unfortunately, such that lots of people *do* let books get badly overdue. Rather than pay, say, a fine of £2.00 (which might not be much short of the purchase price) some people will brazenly attack the computer for sending all those reminders for a book they have 'never seen'. The library staff will need every confidence in the automated systems if they are to call the bluff.

? **Q 16.24** Computer centre staff must classify each book, i.e. assign a Dewey Decimal Number and mark this on the spine; catalogue the book i.e. assign a book number (assuming the library uses its own numbering system and does not just use ISBNs); prepare the book i.e. stamp it with the library's possession stamp and stick in the library's sticker (with space for date-stamping, as in the manual system. They must also prepare a bar code so that the book number may be machine read (there are large typewriter-like machines that will do this, 'typing' a bar code instead of letters and numbers) and stick that into the book.

The recipient library has only to put the book on the shelf.

? **Q 16.25** The librarians must load the machine with information on reserved books, blacklisted readers etc. sent by the computer centre that morning. They must either key in or load with special bar codes the code for that library and whether the light pen is to note issues or returns. They must test that the system is working, including testing that the codes are being recorded.

? **Q 16.26** The computer could easily check out the loans master file to find those loans made to a reader with any given membership number. If the library did not have your number, the computer would check the names held in the borrowers master file to find it. It would print the book titles by a quick search through the stock master file, for each relevant book-number.

? **Q 16.27** It would almost certainly be possible to take out a sixth book on another day. Too many people borrow the agreed maximum to set up 'no-more-books' traps for them. But once you had taken *more* than the five, then your number *would* be included in such a trap so you would probably *not* get the seventh and eighth book. The sixth book would trigger the 'no more than five, please' reminder letters that the computer sends out, although the library service may try to save postage by allowing a few days' grace for such a minor transgression of its rules hoping that in the meantime you will return a book or two.

? **Q 16.28** An on-line system would allow direct interrogation of all files. There would be no need for microfiche catalogues, cassettes etc. Information made available would be up-to-the-minute, allowing, for example, an immediate check on a borrower's book limit.

? **Q 16.29** A library service would want to record the number of times a book is borrowed so that it can see of which titles it might be worth buying extra copies. To do so the book stock master file must include a field for 'number of times borrowed' and the software must arrange for this to be incremented with each loan.

Finding those titles out more than 30 times or less than three times in the course of a year would then involve a simple search of the book-stock master file.

This has been an important development for authors. They are now paid a small royalty according to the number of times that their book has been borrowed from one of some 20 large libraries. This problem of Public Lending Rights has taken some 40 years to be resolved and the solution depends heavily on computer records for its implementation.

? **Q 16.30** Similarly, if a library wished it could arrange software to record the book-number of every title ever loaned to you. This would be expensive on storage space and would considerably slow up processing, but it is possible. Computerisation has meant that innocent procedures can become *so* efficient that they could be used for purposes well beyond the original intentions of the designers.

The librarians themselves are well aware of the dangers; they have recently drafted a code of conduct and know better than to tempt others by collating such information in the first place.

However, it is glib to say that such details, if they existed, would never be used. What would *you* do if you were the chief librarian of your county and George Cowley of CI5 turns up in your office wanting pointers that might confirm that a foreign 'student' is in fact none other than a member of the murderous Bader-Meinhoff terrorist group . . .

If that is somewhat melodramatic, what if your library service is short of money and is approached by a well known and highly reputable supermarket chain that wishes to buy a list of names and addresses of people who have taken out books on home improvements and DIY. The supermarket is about to open a new hypermarket and wants to launch its new home improvements department by sending generous money-off vouchers to handymen in the area.

The library will make money and the readers will benefit from the vouchers. The supermarket will very effectively advertise its new department to precisely those people most likely to use it.

17 Banks

This chapter may well be a rather difficult one for the average GCSE pupil to grasp; few (if any) will have direct experience of running bank accounts (beyond those held at the Post Office or with a building society) whereas they all should have used libraries and supermarkets.

Nevertheless it is very much within the scope of GCSE to teach these 'life skill' aspects of a subject at appropriate times and this application of computing is simply too important to omit.

We suggest that a general discussion of banks and banking might usefully precede the pupils' reading of the chapter. We have included several general banking questions (Q 17.1 to 17.4) to promote this approach.

DISCUSSION POINTS

? **Q 17.1** Not all banks are clearing banks offering cheque accounts that work in the way described. The 'big four' are Barclays, Lloyd's, Midland (which also owns the Northern Bank) and National Westminster.

The other clearing banks are: Coutts & Co., Bank of Scotland, Clydesdale Bank and The Royal Bank of Scotland (which on 1st October 1985 dropped the name Williams and Glyn's that it had previously used for its branches in England).

The Co-Operative Bank, the Trustees Savings Bank and and the National Girobank (run by the Post Office), although not regarded as traditional 'clearing banks', have nevertheless joined the clearing system.

Other banks that the students may know (most notably the Bank of England) are *not* cheque clearing banks.

? **Q 17.2** (*a*) Current account—cheque account; usually no interest paid on money held there; overdrafts possible

(*b*) Deposit account—interest paying savings account

(*c*) Cheque card—guarantees payment on a cheque (up to the £50 limit)

(*d*) Cash card—works the cash dispensing machines

(*e*) Credit card—like Access or Visa, enables holder to buy now and pay later

(*f*) Credit slip—paying-in slip

(*g*) Standing order—regular, fixed payment made automatically

(*h*) Direct debit—similar in principal to a standing order, except that the recipient (i.e. the TV rental company or whatever) can vary the amount collected.

? **Q 17.4** Although many retail businesses will handle considerable quantities of cash at their sales end, they will probably only make one cash deposit in the course of the day. The rest of their business will be conducted on the basis of cheques (to pay their suppliers) and automatic payments (to pay salaries and/or collect regular HP or rental instalments by direct debit from the customers' accounts). Businesses *not* in the retail trade are unlikely to use much cash at all unless they pay weekly wages as cash.

? **Q 17.5** The banks agreed to standardise their cheque codes from 1962 and so there is a long-standing (and considerable) investment in MICR. Magnetic ink character recognition has two vital advantages over OCR; namely accuracy and security. Credits, however, include a mixture of MICR and ordinary line-printed characters (that are both alpha and numeric). Magnetic ink readers and sorters can only read numerics and for this reason OCR is preferred (OCR fonts include alpha symbols). Both systems can read at about 2000 documents per minute and so there is no loss of speed.

The banks are not able to control the paper and print specifications of credits as tightly as they can those of cheques, for others also issue credit slips. Look at your gas or electricity bill for an example.

? **Q 17.6** A branch must have at least a 'dumb' terminal on-line to the central computer. (In fact, of course, most branches have considerably better equipment than this.)

If the branch were not on-line, it could not inspect the accounts of its own customers, nor process its own cheques, nor stop payment on wrongly drafted cheques on day three of the clearing process.

? **Q 17.7** The computer centre must have a large mainframe capable of simultaneously handling many transactions to and from many sources: the branch terminals, the cheque readers and sorters and keyboards in the computer centre, its own extensive disc and tape storage systems and so on. There must be facilities for very rapid print-out of statements (using the latest laser printers, the banks can now print over 8000 statements per hour) and for the long term storage of banking records (computer output on microfilm etc.).

? **Q 17.8** In one sense centralised information is easier to secure; there is only one place to protect.

However, if disaster were to strike then everything could be lost. The banks go to enormous lengths to ensure their systems are 'fail-safe' and so there is virtually no chance of losing details of a customer's account by routine accident. Naturally they keep the previous day's master files and the relevant transactions files separate from the current master files (see Chapter 10) and back-up copies of all vital files. Earthquakes, fires and terrorist attacks *do* happen, nevertheless and so the banks do not keep all their information in one place. 'Just in case', they swop information between two or more centres, usually daily.

? **Q 17.9** If an organisation is to use BACS it must, naturally, have computerised its own procedures, although it need not own a computer (if it uses a bureau). Typically, a company using BACS would have a staff of over 250 to which it pays salaries once a month and/or many customers paying insurance premiums; HP instalments; TV rental etc. by monthly direct debit.

Every major organisation in the UK now uses BACS. Thus local authorities pay their salaried staff and collect rates (for those who wish to pay monthly) through BACS. The TV licensing authority collects monthly instalments this way, as do the gas and electricity boards and British Telecom. Three quarters of life assurance premiums are collected through BACS. Annual payments such as union dues, AA and RAC membership, donations to charity etc. are also collected this way. The list is *very* extensive. Nearly half a million wages are also paid, every week, through this automatic system.

Administrative costs, not least, bank charges, are reduced for the customer and the banks' own procedures are considerably simplified. Unquestionably, more and more payments will be made this way—probably over half of all transactions by the early 1990s.

? **Q 17.10** The banks will only allow a company access to BACS if they are sure of the firm's secure financial standing and credit worthiness. They also insist that any direct debit may be reclaimed—automatically, of course—as soon as the bank (or, more usually, the customer) notices an error.

? **Q 17.12** The card must carry, at the barest minimum, the customer's account number, branch and PIN.

? **Q 17.13** If the bank's ATMs go off-line 'after hours', then there must be an additional computer system to keep track of the transactions made overnight. This subsidiary computer must contains its own file of customer details, namely PIN and maximum withdrawal limit. It may *not* be able to give the customer an up-to-date balance or to print out a statement, as can those machines permanently on-line to the central computer. It can, however, note requests for statements, new cheque books etc.

Since the ATMs are on-line to a subsidiary computer network, it should not be possible to defraud the bank by making large withdrawals at different machines. In any case, it is usual for the magnetic strip code to include a weekly withdrawal limit and the ATM to record the date of the card's last use and the amount withdrawn.

? **Q 17.14** If the banks are to allow customers of other banks to use their cash dispensing facility then it is essential that their coding systems and machines are compatible with each other. (In fact, the machines used in the UK are almost all made by one of two companies, NCR or IBM, and so this is not a problem.)

As one bank does not have access to the other's customers' accounts, it cannot at any time know the balance in an account. So it is *essential* that the magnetic strip code includes a weekly withdrawal limit and that the ATM records how much cash is withdrawn and when.

It would be possible to offer a full range of services to the other's customers only if the banking service was virtually integrated (in which case the banks could merge with each other). Requests for statements etc. might be allowed, but access to customers' account details implies a direct on-line link and unrestricted use of the other's computer.

Midland and National Westminster first established a 'reciprocity' agreement in 1983. Barclays, Lloyd's, the Bank of Scotland and the Royal Bank of Scotland now allow their customers to use each others' machines as well. But members of the public have to be careful because a Nat West card will *not* operate a Lloyd's machine, and vice versa. The banks themselves readily admit that it will be years before they fully integrate their networks of ATMs.

? **Q 17.15** Establishing EFTPOS will take time, for a number of significant problems must be overcome. In particular there will be considerable initial expense (and inconvenience) in establishing the necessary cable networks throughout the country. The Government has supported a number of experiments, in the first instance relating to cable TV, but there has been local resistance (to dug up roads, junction boxes above ground spoiling 'scenic' views etc.) and financial snares (Rediffusion pulled out after a year or two from franchises granted to it in Guildford, for example).

Retailers may well resist taking up EFTPOS links unless the banks considerably subsidise the installation costs, or they calculate that EFTPOS will lead to a significant increase in trade. There will be some political battles too. The banks are happy to allow the credit card companies access to their EFTPOS terminals (after all, they themselves are heavily involved with running the Access and Visa operations) but will not take kindly to building society involvement.

Probably, it will be the biggest retailers who first involve themselves. The corner shops may feel unable to afford the installation costs until such time as they can no longer resist so popular a service. (Exactly this happened with credit cards: although even now there are still plenty of shops who will not take them.) Probably, the building societies *will* be excluded (although the retailers *would* like to see them involved; if Joe Public has easier access to his savings account, he is more likely to spend the money).

? **Q 17.16** (*a*) *Banks. Advantages:* (i) reduced paperwork; (ii) reduced day-to-day bank costs; (iii) casual fraud reduced (any amateur thief can forge a signature on a cheque or credit card voucher but he cannot use a cash card without the PIN); (iv) likely significantly to increase the numbers of people holding bank accounts; (v) reduced cash movement.

Disadvantages: (i) expensive to set up; (ii) security must be elaborate to fend off professional criminals (who could make 'a killing' if they were to succeed).

(*b*) *Shops. Advantages:* (i) faster check-out procedures (cheque and credit card sales are slow and bureaucratic); (ii) immediate payment; (iii) tills maintained accurately (most till operators, however careful and honest, make some errors in the course of the day); (iv) opportunities for staff pilfering of cash reduced; (v) no large sums of cash to deposit at end of day's trading (when banks are shut); (vi) accounting procedures simplified; (vii) internal administrative costs and bank charges reduced.

Disadvantages: (i) expensive to instal (and so likely to accelerate trend away from corner shops); (ii) technical failure could be disastrous.

(*c*) *Customers. Advantages:* (i) convenience—no need to carry cash, or to visit bank to get it; (ii) security—lost cash is lost, but no casual thief can use a lost card without knowing the PIN. In any case once the bank is informed that the card is missing no-one could use it.

Disadvantages: (i) payment is immediate—no 3-day period of grace as with a cheque; (ii) keeping track of spending and the balance left in the account will be difficult (and could lead to embarrassing situations at the checkout).

? **Q 17.17** The larger banks and building societies already have customers in most parts of the country using their networks of thousands of local branches (sometimes several in any one town).

Since it would be extremely expensive for them to attempt to set up a similar chain of local offices, it is logical for the smaller banks and building societies to try to reach into new areas using the new technology.

However, the Midland Bank has also 'dabbled' in home banking but not with the high-profile advertising campaign of the Bank of Scotland.

? **Q 17.18** The use of cheques is likely to be *substantially* reduced if not eliminated altogether in the longer term when home banking is well established (so that private individuals can transfer money to each other) and *every* corner shop has an EFTPOS terminal.

? **Q 17.19** There will almost certainly continue to be a use for cash, however. Small purchases (a bus ticket, a newspaper, sweets for the children) will be made in cash. Those without bank accounts (children, for example, must learn how to handle money well before they could possibly cope with a bank account) will be excluded from the electronic systems. And the 'black economy' (not an insignificant part of modern life providing possibly as much of 10% of Britain's total income) depends upon its 'cash only' maxim.

18 Schools

DISCUSSION POINTS

? **Q 18.1** We have included this question in order to remind students just how expensive the initial capital requirement is to set up a properly equipped computer room that can service a whole class.

We do not really expect students to be able to give much of an answer to the question 'Where did the money come from?' but as teachers we feel some discussion on the matter is worthwhile; too many young people take school equipment for granted. They *ought* to know whether or not the PTA was involved in the initial purchases of their school's computers; if they do not, there is all the more reason for reminding them.

Under the Department of Trade and Industry's initial scheme a 50% subsidy was payable on three computers: The Research Machines 380Z (that then cost around £3000 making the subsidy worth £1500) the Acorn/BBC machine (that then cost £399 so making the subsidy worth £200) and the Sinclair Spectrum (costing then £125, so making the subsidy worth £62.50).

This pound-for-pound approach had the effect of involving many parent/teacher associations, who, to their credit, were highly successful in raising the funds. In the first year of the scheme 80% of Britain's 6500+ secondary schools had raised the money to buy at least one microcomputer.

Many schools bought the 380Z (it seemed the better deal and could obviously run more elaborate educational software than the original 32K BBC) only to find that they had then committed themselves to a far greater computer power than they knew how to use. Six or seven smaller computers would surely have been the better buy.

In the authors' view, the educationalists made the classic error that has similarly beset many others launching into computing for the first time, namely buying the hardware and only *then* working out what to do with it.

In fairness, given the shortage of teachers trained in computing, most head teachers had little or no local advice on which they could depend.

? **Q 18.2** Again this is rather hard for students to answer in any detail, but if they have understood this course they should have learned to question the adequacy of three key factors crucial to the success of any new application of computers: the software, the hardware and the preparation of staff.

Putting at least one computer into every school in so short a time was an achievement. And to incorporate this initiative into a wider campaign (involving well established institutions such as the BBC and the NEC and giving two fledgling UK microcomputer manufacturing companies such a flying start), and at the same time to begin pioneering experiments with telesoftware, was commendably forward-looking, bold even.

● BUT was it right to establish BASIC so firmly in British schools? The Danish scheme centres around a Danish built computer that uses a better structured language, a hybrid of Pascal and BASIC, called COMAL 80. Eire and Norway are now following the Danish example. Acorn built the computer to meet the BBC's specification; it could easily have carried a different resident language, as could the 380Z. (In fact, a COMAL chip has been available from Acorn for some years.)

● BUT one solitary computer in a school is nothing like enough. If a class is to use the computer as a central part of a lesson there should be *at least a dozen* of them.

● BUT what were the teachers expected to make of it? Apart from a small number of recent graduates in mathematics and sciences—mostly inexperienced teachers—almost all school staff were completely untrained in using microcomputers. (Two-day familiarisation courses were organised for a small number of teachers, but that hardly constitutes proper training.)

Contrast this with the French initiative, heavily influenced by Seymour Papert, author of LOGO and just about *the* world authority on computers in education. The French have given teacher training much the highest priority; every school in the country has had to second two teachers for a year-long in-service training course. However France has not been as fast as the UK to introduce the hardware. The '10 000 computers' project came to fruition in September 1986. But by then the 1250 + lycées of France will each have (in addition to other computers bought outside the scheme) a net of at least eight microcomputers with appropriate peripherals and at least two properly trained teachers to run it.

? **Q 18.3** This question was set in order to allow students to figure for themselves much of what follows—and allow teachers the opportunity to discuss the constraints under which they operate in their particular school.

Our 'Ten Strengths' have been freely adapted from 14 'Principal Advantages of Computer-Based Learning' discussed in *The Three Cs: Children, Computers and Communication*, by Tom Stonier and Cathy Conlin (Wiley, 1985) which we would regard as essential reading for *anyone* involved with education (not just computer education) whether teacher, parent or theoretician.

? **Q 18.4** The keyboard is a barrier between some young children and the computer (for some adults too). Touch tablets and so on are an ideal alternative for young children (see Chapter 5).

? **Q 18.5** The point here is best illustrated by the airline-pilots' training simulator; there are no dead bodies and no dents in expensive aircraft should the trainee make a disastrous mistake. (Should car drivers be trained in a similar way?)

A scientific or statistical experiment at school may be too expensive, too dangerous or simply impractical to carry out, but it may be easily simulated on a computer.

? **Q 18.6** 'Training' is a narrow exercise preparing ('programming'?) someone for a specific job or task. CBT systems are already working.

'Education' implies something considerably wider. CBE is still some years off.

? **Q 18.7** We are not trying to train 16-year-olds to be teachers but we think it a good exercise for older children to comment on the educational software intended for their younger brothers and sisters. It is likely that they will have more 'feel' for this than attempts of evaluating business or other software intended for the adult world in which, for all our efforts to prepare them for it, they have yet to move.

Obviously what you can demonstrate will depend upon what software you have. Have you thought of approaching a local 'feeder' middle or primary school and exchanging comments and ideas?

? **Q 18.9, Q 18.10** and **Q 18.11** The Hertfordshire Computer Managed Mathematics Project deliberately includes some teacher-marked assignments to ensure that every pupil must, at some point, seek teacher contact.

The possibility of some pupils not enjoying an adequate share of the teacher's time is an obvious disadvantage of the scheme. Class size is crucial.

A great deal also depends on the skill with which the subject matter is presented on the video tapes and worksheets.

On the whole, however, such a scheme ought to ensure more individual contact and discussion between teacher and taught, especially as the teacher is freed from the marking and record keeping (no more than clerical work) of the job. The pupils can work at their own pace assured of work that is within their capabilities. They enjoy the status of using the computer.

? **Q 18.12** The advantages are those of any electronic mail system, namely easy access to a wealth of (educational) software and the TTNS data bank as well as the speed and reliability of communication; circulars to several schools in the area or in a whole county (or even in the whole country) can be distributed very readily.

The disadvantages are (i) the need to keyboard all correspondence (accepted business practice of course but not automatic in the education world) and (ii) the likely prospect of unauthorised and/or juvenile use.

(Some electronic mail companies have a 'naughty words editor' built into their computer systems. Messages containing offensive words or phrases are not 'posted' to the recipient's mailbox but, instead, are automatically directed to an 'abeyance' file where they are only forwarded *after* they have been visually checked by the mail service staff and found acceptable.)

? **Q 18.14** A daisy-wheel (letter quality) printer and at least a single disk drive would be essential. Dual disk drives (with appropriate back-up procedures) would be desirable.

? **Q 18.15** (*a*) Change 'fourth' to 'fifth' throughout. Change day and date of meeting (and time if necessary). Delete from list of teachers those who teach the fourth but not the fifth; insert names of teachers who teach the fifth but not the fourth.

(*b*) Changes to the letter would probably be made by editing text on the screen, although a change that requires 'fourth' to become 'fifth' wherever it occurs could be achieved by a single edit command on most word processors. The list of teachers could also be edited on screen, but if the details of the classes each teacher takes are kept on a computer file, the list could be automatically extracted from that (see 'databases', Chapter 19).

(*c*) The accuracy and presentation of all typewritten material emanating from the head teacher's office and the speed with which he or she could expect it to be completed would improve no matter how competent the secretaries on their ordinary typewriters. The head teacher would feel more able to insist on minor alterations to any letter about to be signed (word processing for their secretaries has had this effect on most business executives). The head teacher might be able, given the saving of time, to extend the secretarial service to other activities in the school (notably for the typing of some teaching materials).

(*d*) The secretaries would find their work a lot less pressured and much of the tedium of retyping letters and lists for a few small changes would be eliminated. They might well, however, feel that their jobs were being threatened.

? **Q 18.16** Cost. Also, many head teachers are only very vaguely aware of the advantages word processing might bring. There would be no immediate financial advantages to county authorities (unless they make some secretaries redundant).

? **Q 18.17** Many teaching staff do a lot of typing of worksheets, examination papers etc. Not being professional typists they tend to make a good number of keyboard slips (the authors do). A word processor in the staff room would make the initial typing and subsequent updating and correction of old worksheets and examination papers very easy. It would also encourage teachers to pay closer attention to the presentation quality of the worksheets they produce. (Again, this has been the authors' first-hand experience.) It would also help teachers from all disciplines to become confident in using computers so increasing the likelihood of their use *in* the classroom.

? **Q 18.18** Senior school students now have to present, for formal assessment and moderation, large quantities of coursework in their GCSE subjects (not least in this one). The ready availability of word processing facilities would have much the same effect on them as it would on the teaching staff, i.e. it would help them to type, continually correct and redraft what they have written. It would encourage them to pay much closer attention to the quality of their overall presentation. It would help those as yet unsure about computers to become familiar with them, and, at the end of the day, it would enable them to submit something which was genuinely their best effort.

Seymour Papert argues for using word processors with *junior* schoolchildren too, and for much the same reasons. So long as the child (who might be, say, ten years old) can write and use a keyboard, the word processor would encourage the child to correct anything that was even slightly wrong and to revise continually what he or she has already written. All this would cause the child to develop the habit of reading and re-reading his own work with a view to criticising and correcting it, while still making possible a high-quality presentation that otherwise eludes all but a few clever children. This continual review and improvement is in itself a valuable habit that, currently, even much older children (and some adults) lack. Furthermore, the lack of quality in the handwritten presentation achievable by most children would cease to be a barrier between them and the (non-language related) issues they are trying to write about; they would be able to concentrate on the *content*.

? **Q 18.19** The school would probably keep a *subjects file* something like that shown in the text; there may in fact be more detail than that kept in the computer, e.g. mathematics is tested at three levels at GCSE, and there is no provision for recording that in the file shown.

Year of Entry (2)	Reference Number (3)	Surname (20)	First Name (15)	Second Name (15)	Third Name (15)	Known as (15)	PUPIL DETAILS
Form (2)	Form Tutor (3)	Previous School (20)	Male/ Female (1)	Date of Birth (6)	Doctor's Name (20)	Doctor's Tel (12)	
Address Line 1 (20)	Address Line 2 (20)	Address Line 3 (20)	Address Line 4 (20)	Address Line 5 (20)	Telephone Number (12)		PUPIL'S ADDRESS
Father's Initials (3)	Mother's Initials (3)	Father's Work Tel (12)	Mother's Work Tel (12)	Correspondence Addressed to: (10)			PARENTS' DETAILS
English (4, 3, 2, 1)	Maths (4, 3, 2, 1)	Option A (4, 3, 2, 1)	Option B (4, 3, 2, 1)	Option C (4, 3, 2, 1)	Option D (4, 3, 2, 1)	Option E (4, 3, 2, 1)	GCSE SUBJECTS; TEACHER; EXAM YEAR; GRADE
Monday 1 (4, 2)	Monday 2 (4, 2,)	Monday 3 (4, 2)	Monday 4 (4, 2)	Monday 5 (4, 2)	Tuesday 1 (4, 2)		TIMETABLE: SUBJECT; ROOM

Fig. 18.1 (*a*) Barchester Comprehensive School's pupil file layout

The *pupils file* would include all the pupils in the school. This application needs an extracted file for third year pupils (since this is the year the options are chosen).

83	009	Brown	Samantha	Anne	—	Sam
4R	WHR	Green Park First	F	080872	Dr Roberts	Bar 59372
44, Kingsway	Barchester	Newshire	BA61 2NN	—	Bar 45678	
PQ	RS	01-889 -1660	Bar 87654	Mr and Mrs		
Engl SRD 88 —	Math JSF 88 —	Fren FAO 88 —	Comp JSF 88 —	Busi DES 88 —	Biol JWM 88 —	Hist RGM 88 —
Math 24	Busi 18	French 3	Biol BL	Hist 17	PE —	

Fig. 18.2 (*b*) Barchester Comprehensive School's record on Samantha Brown (a fourth-year pupil) as at February 1987

The details included would be at least those shown in Fig. 18.1.

? **Q 18.20** The form might be input from a mark sense card. An optical mark reader now costs only a few hundred pounds. The form shown presumes this (see Fig. 18.3).

Validation checks would include a range check for the pupil's identity number and a check that the number of choices was correct (i.e. one in each timetable group).

? **Q 18.21** The basic structure of the timetable (i.e. the number of lessons per day and how they are grouped into 'blocks'), the number of subjects, the lessons required for each subject and the options timetable against each other (e.g. a school may deliberately timetable European studies against French since it runs the former as an alternative course for those unable to cope with the latter), the subject teachers, the teaching load for each etc.

Each school has many special requirements, e.g. for part-time staff, those teachers prepared to take a small number of games lessons etc. In fact the timetable details will vary greatly from school to school.

It would be sensible to illustrate this computing application by using your own school's timetable.

BARCHESTER COMPREHENSIVE SCHOOL FOURTH YEAR OPTIONS

Name.. Reference Number | 8 | 7 | | | |

Fill ONE ☐ in each column with a *black* pen as shown: ■

Ask your Form Teacher what to do if you are in any doubt or if you make a mistake or change your mind.

YOUR REF NUMBER (It appears on the top of this form if you have forgotten it)					
		0 ☐	0 ☐	0 ☐	0 ☐
		1 ☐	1 ☐	1 ☐	1 ☐
		2 ☐	2 ☐	2 ☐	2 ☐
		3 ☐	3 ☐	3 ☐	3 ☐
		4 ☐	4 ☐	4 ☐	4 ☐
		5 ☐	5 ☐	5 ☐	5 ☐
		6 ☐	6 ☐	6 ☐	6 ☐
		7 ■	7 ☐	7 ☐	7 ☐
	8 ■	8 ☐	8 ☐	8 ☐	8 ☐
	9 ☐	9 ☐	9 ☐	9 ☐	9 ☐

YOUR CHOICES — You have to make ONE choice in each block.

BLOCK A	BLOCK B	BLOCK C	BLOCK D	BLOCK E
French ☐	French ☐	French ☐	French ☐	German ☐
Europn St ☐	Geog ☐	Spanish ☐	Geog ☐	Geology ☐
Comp St ☐	Comp St ☐	Physics ☐	Physics ☐	Elctrncs ☐
Biology ☐	Chem ☐	Chem ☐	Biology ☐	History ☐
Metalwk ☐	CDT ☐	CDT ☐	Metalwk ☐	CDT ☐
Gra Com ☐	Gra Com ☐	Woodwk ☐	Woodwk ☐	Art/Des ☐
Music ☐	Drama ☐	Art ☐	Art ☐	Commerce ☐
Home Ec ☐	Govt & Pol ☐	Bus St ☐	Accounts ☐	Econ ☐

English, Maths, PE, Religious Education and Preparation for Living are NOT options. They automatically appear on your timetable next year.
Some combinations of subjects are not permitted—refer to your Options Notes.

Fig. 18.3 Barchester Comprehensive School's input form for fourth-year options

? **Q 18.22** It is very likely that the computer will *not* find an ideal solution that meets everyone's requirements. In that case, compromises have to be made, just as if the timetabling was manually controlled.

? **Q 18.23** The school's pupils (or students) file would usually include each individual's reference number, name, sex, date of birth, form, address, telephone number, parents' name(s) and second address if appropriate, previous school, house (if appropriate) and subjects taken. Many other details may be considered appropriate by a particular school and most software for schools allows room for many more additional fields.

? **Q 18.25** Schools (in fact the local education authority for the maintained sector) have had to register under the Data Protection Act if they hold computerised files. Some information may be sensitive, especially to those pupils whose parents have split up. Even examination grades should really be a private matter between an individual and his teachers.

Of course, these details are already held in most schools, whether or not the records have been computerised. The threat to privacy arises as much from the efficiency with which computerised files may be manipulated and 'posted' (electronically) to other authorities (see Chapter 22) as from the data held.

? **Q 18.27** Probably not. Classroom requirements are different from administrative ones (e.g. good colour graphics are essential for the classroom).

Administrative computers need much larger storage capacity and fast processing speed but do not need colour monitors.

If the computer systems are completely separate, then the security problems are considerably eased. Some senior staff who function in both administrative and teaching rôles would have to learn how to handle two separate systems however.

The addresses of the publishers of schools software included in this chapter are included on page 141.

JIIG-CAL is an acronym for Jobs, Ideas and Information Generator-Computer Assisted Learning.

19 What If . . .?

DISCUSSION POINTS

? **Q 19.1** Computer modelling, like many 'real-life' applications, will be far from most students' experience. This question is intended to encourage an understanding of the diversity of models and of their purposes.

Students should think of some of these examples without prompting:

Model	Purpose
Train set/cars/aeroplanes/toy soldiers/ dolls etc.	Create fantasy worlds or 'copy' the real world
Duck decoys	Fool other ducks
Model villages/waxworks like Madame Tussaud's	Entertainment
Museum models; e.g. engines/ processes	Education/demonstration
Skeletons/human organs	Education/training
Product models	Sales (often before product is made!)
Fragile artifacts or monuments e.g. the full size replica of the Lascaux caves	Preserve or reconstruct the original/ tourism/education
Graven images	Worship/idolatry/voodoo

? **Q 19.2** The *assumptions* built into the model may be incorrect; e.g. the air-flow might be more turbulent on a *real* runway or the *real* brick wall might be stronger, causing worse injuries etc.

Vehicle, ship and aeroplane designers have to be very careful: a model's behaviour *can* be quite different from a full-size version!

? **Q 19.3** Yes and no. They certainly fully *represent* the third dimension with accurate contours, perspective and shading. However, they *display* the models via a 2-dimensional medium, the VDU screen. As usual, somebody is working on it. Fully 3-D display media (using techniques such as holography) are on the way.

? **Q 19.4** Such models can easily be rescaled to put any size or shape of person 'in the driving seat' (or any other workspace). The SAMMIE system, in fact, stores statistical data on the distribution of different heights, reaches etc. among the real population. For each sized version of SAMMIE, the designer can even 'become' the model, seeing the controls, instruments and views in the mirrors exactly as that driver would.

? **Q 19.5** Spreadsheets come into their own only when the figures are reasonably complex and are likely to change with changed assumptions (as in this example). This is a good time to remind students not to use the computer just because it is there but because it will save time and/or improve the accuracy of the information used.

(*a*) Income and expenditure are never smoothly spread over the whole year and so annual totals cannot show the profit or loss in a given month. For example, there are no ticket sales in July (the football season has not begun) so the manager (*and the club's bank*) must be prepared for a significant loss which will be made up in the winter months. December is the best month for Barchester United; they play several home games and fundraising (draws etc.) is especially successful in the run up to Christmas.

(*b*) This is sometimes done but this level of detail is usually too much; general patterns cannot be seen from too little *or* from too much data.

(*c*) Electricity is, of course, used in every month (although more heavily in winter for heating and floodlighting) but it is actually *billed* (just like at home) every quarter.

This means, incidentally, that the figures shown here do not, strictly speaking, reflect profit and loss but *flows of cash* into and out of the club. This important accounting distinction may be ignored at this level unless time and ability permit.

? **Q 19.6** (*a*) Fig. 19.10 shows the expenditure figures only for the last quarter of the year (April-June) plus the total expenditure (column N).

(*b*) The planned payment for rent and rates in May (cell L19).

? **Q 19.7** B24 contains the formula SUM(B15:B22)
B11 contains the formula SUM(B7:B9)
D9 does *not* contain a formula,
just the value 15 000
E26 contains the formula SUBTRACT (E11:E24)

? **Q 19.8** Spreadsheets tend to remain confusing until students have had direct experience. Their own finances are a sensible application for a first attempt; encourage them to use their own real figures rather than copy the fastest student's version.

(*c*) Some students will realise that cash flow is involved again here. A 'loss' means depleting money in your pocket or savings (assets), while a 'profit' means the reverse. If someone does not have enough money at the start of the week to finance an expected loss, they must either boost income (earn, scrounge or borrow more) or cut expenditure (resist that new record etc.). No doubt some students will have 'interest on savings' as one of their sources of income.

Simulation Exercise

This exercise will rapidly give students a practical insight into simulation. The only 'computing' equipment required is a die! More ambitious students, if time permits, will want to attempt a more lifelike simulation, but this will require more advanced programming skills.

Possible factors for a full simulation:

- One or more checkouts breaking down
- Items that are unpriced (or have bar codes missing)
- Replacement of damaged items
- Fresh foods (might have to be priced or weighed at the checkout)
- Different payment methods (cash, cheques, credit cards)
- Physical length of queues (which can block the aisles)
- Availability of baskets and trolleys
- Peak shopping hours
- 'Express' checkouts for cash customers with no more than six items.

Time (minutes)	Event	Time at checkout	Total people at checkout
0			
1			
2			
3			
4			
5			
6			
7			
8			
9			
10			
11			
12			
13			
14			
15			
16			
17			
18			
19			
20			
21			
22			
23			
24			
25			
26			
27			
28			
29			
30			

Fig. 19.1 Worksheet for Supermarket Checkout Simulation

You might get some groups to measure some of the variables at a real supermarket—but see the manager first!

Materials required: Photocopies of simulation worksheets

Dice (one per team of 2–3 students)

Briefing: A survey at the Barchester Superstore has shown that approximately 30 shoppers pass through each checkout per hour. The time taken for their shopping to be checked and paid for varies from one to six minutes.

A simulation is needed of the queue at *one* checkout only. Students may assume that (a) shoppers arrive at the checkout at a steady rate of one every two minutes, and (b) time at the checkout varies randomly—a die can be rolled to give the time (in minutes) for each customer.

Students should record the results of their simulations (we suggest working in teams of two or three) on a blank worksheet. You can explain how to use the worksheet by running through the sample simulation given below:

Time (min)	Event	Time (min) at checkout*	Total people at checkout
0	Customer 1 arrives	1	1
1	Customer 1 leaves		0
2	Customer 2 arrives	4	1
3			1
4	Customer 3 arrives	6	2
5			2
6	2 leaves/4 arrives	5	2
7			2
8	5 arrives	4	3
9			3
10	3 leaves/6 arrives	2	3
etc. . . .			

*from score on die

Each team should run their simulation for 30 'minutes'. You can then discuss the range of results, worst case, and so on. The exercise can be repeated with different assumptions (try doubling the time at the checkout) to see how the queues would be affected. See worksheet on page 95.

? **Q 19.9** If the model is inaccurate, students could actually learn to administer dangerous treatments that might help the computer 'patient' but harm a real one. For this reason MacPuff was carefully tested, comparing simulator results with the behaviour of real patients in intensive care; a very high correlation was found, confirming the validity of the model.

? **Q 19.10** Scientific and technical applications may spring to mind but there is scope for simulation to educate and/or train people in areas as diverse as history, nature conservation, management, music and politics. Some suppliers of simulation software for microcomputers are given on pages 136–41 of this Guide.

Q 19.11 'Hard' evidence of the climatic effects of all-out nuclear war is obviously unavailable and so simulation *must* be taken seriously. The original study (by Richard Turco *et al.*) has been followed up by several more. The most thorough simulation, carried out by the Scientific Committee on Problems of the Environment (SCOPE), used an interactive 3-D model of the world's climate. It confirmed the earlier findings: the nuclear winter would almost certainly be prolonged.

We have grim evidence from Hiroshima and Nagasaki of the nature of direct nuclear casualties, but indirect victims would probably be even more numerous. The SCOPE simulation also predicted massive crop failure and drought as extremely likely consequences. Noncombatant countries like India and China would be major indirect victims. Overall, the SCOPE team suggested that natural ecosystems could support *less than one per cent* of the world's present population.

20 In Control

DISCUSSION POINTS

Q 20.1

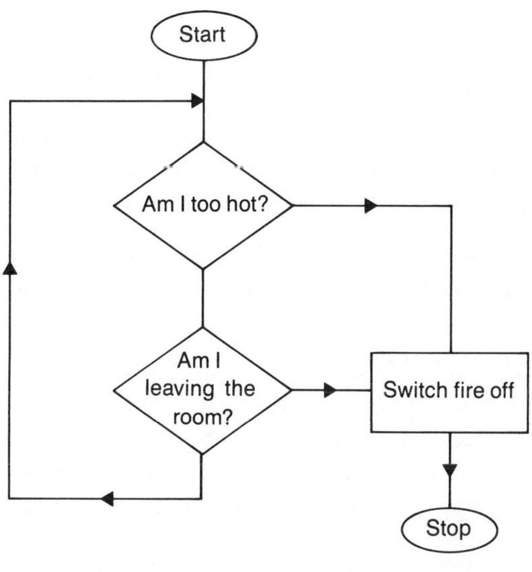

The figure on page 97 assumes the fire is on to start with; it would be more useful if it also covered the opposite case. There might be other circumstances with which it could not cope, e.g. other people (with different ideas as to a comfortable temperature) in the room, doctor's orders to keep the fire on, such bitter cold outside that keeping the fire on will barely maintain the temperature etc.

? **Q 20.2**

(*a*) Examples of 'blind' control:

(i) Older record players have styli (or needles) that are lowered to the turntable at a preset position, even though the record may be of the wrong size.

(ii) Some milkmen continue to deliver a 'standing order' of, say, two pints *irrespective* of full bottles collecting on the doorstep when people on holiday forget to stop deliveries.

(iii) Traffic light controllers with fixed intervals (may make a motorist wait even though no-one else is at the junction).

(iv) Watering plants daily *without* checking if they are waterlogged.

(*b*) Examples of 'closed loop' control:

(i) Modern record decks that sense the size of record before lowering the stylus.

(ii) The milkman who uses feedback. Seeing yesterday's full bottles still on the doorstep, he stops deliveries until the position is clarified.

(iii) Traffic lights with sensors (usually under the road) to modify their operation sequence.

(iv) Self-watering plant pots that 'sense' when an absorbent wick is drying out (usually using capillary action to draw up more water); or the gardener who checks the soil for moistness before watering.

? **Q 20.3** For walking or picking up a pen we use feedback, conscious or unconscious, from the muscles (information examples: your right foot is about to touch the ground, you are gripping the pen firmly enough to lift it) and from the eyes (information: the ground level is about to rise or fall, your hand is in position to start the gripping action).

For reading we use feedback from the eyes (e.g. you have reached the end of the line or page), from the eye muscles (e.g. the book is too close, too far away or you are tired), from the brain (e.g. read that sentence again, I didn't understand it) and so on.

Communicating with others, as all teachers know, is most effective when it involves visual (e.g. does he look as though he understands, is she paying attention, is she drawing the diagram correctly) and aural (e.g. is my voice carrying to the back, please explain your answer, can anyone think of another example of . . .) feedback.

? **Q 20.4** We suggest running this exercise as follows: get two volunteers from the class. No. 1 draws the diagram on the board under verbal instruction from No. 2, without speaking at all or turning away from the board. No. 2 should be given a copy of Fig. 20.1 which is to be drawn by No. 1 within, say, five minutes. No. 2 should be at the other end of the room, facing away from the board until the time is up. Observers must keep quiet.

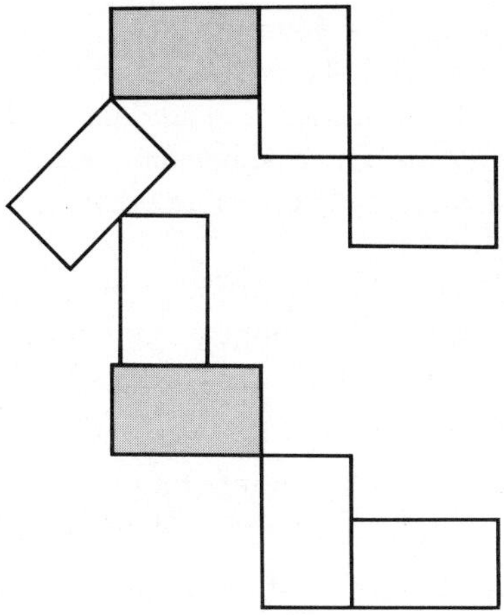

Fig. 20.1

No such restrictions apply to part (*b*). Use different people and allow questions, answers and eye contact (although the instructor should not reveal the diagram, Fig. 20.2, below).

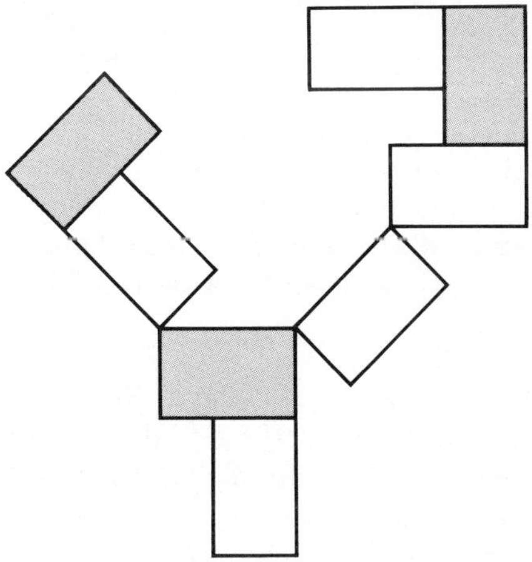

Fig. 20.2

This exercise brings home how much we take feedback for granted in communication; in part (*b*) the drawing is always much more accurate.

[?] **Q 20.5** Without this tolerance zone, the system would switch on and off many more times per day, causing undue wear and tear and possible waste of energy.

[?] **Q 20.6** Automatic control can also be more flexible than human control. Controlling the changing mixture of freight trains, passenger shuttles and express trains that will travel through the Channel Tunnel will require automatic 'drivers' in order to minimise delays.

The biggest advantage is reliability and, as a result, safety. Human operators are far more likely to make mistakes under pressure than a well designed automatic control system. Remind students of Fig. 5.23 in their text, which was designed after the Three Mile Island accident but before the Chernobyl disaster; both involved grave human error.

[?] **Q 20.7** BBC (e.g. Model B, Master 128) I/O connectors:

The analog port is for input only, accepts four analog voltages and has two digital inputs as well.

The user port (which is in fact half of an integrated circuit: the 6522 'versatile interface adaptor' or VIA) can input and output digital signals; it can be set up for input or output from within a BASIC program.

The cassette port is just a small relay (a type of switch) for driving a cassette player, but the small voltage available *can* also be used to activate other devices. The *MOTOR 1 command closes the relay contacts; *MOTOR 0 opens them again. Thus the cassette port can be used for 'digital' output only.

Interfacing circuits are well beyond the scope of GCSE. Any students who do get involved in interfacing projects must be closely supervised to ensure safety (*a*) for themselves, and (*b*) for the microcomputer(s) which can be damaged by inadvertently applying relatively low voltages.

Many teachers will not wish to spend time on hardware design, but would still like to explore control systems with their classes. Fortunately there is now a considerable range of ready-built interface modules, controllers, buggies and robot arms on the market.

[?] **Q 20.8** Because the feedback from the results of the process must be received quickly enough to modify the process itself; this is a *definition* of a real-time system.

[?] **Q 20.9** *Analog-to-digital*: A digital clock or watch can be thought of as converting continuous time to a digital form, some homes have scales, radio tuners and thermometers with digital readouts, converting varying weights, frequencies and temperatures respectively. All cars have a 'digital' odometer, although strictly the 'tenths-of-a-mile' wheel on the mechanical type moves continuously.

Digital-to-analog: Home computers must convert digital signals to analog signals in order to produce any sound (even simple beeps) from their loudspeakers; similarly, compact disc players convert the digital signals (recorded as pits on the disc) to analog form to feed to the amplifier and loudspeakers.

? **Q 20.10** (*a*) For the satellite, distances or bearings (both analog) would have to be measured in order to check the course. The control centre would probably need to know the weight (analog) of fuel remaining, the direction (analog) in which the motor was pointing as well as its status (on/off: digital).

For automatic weighing, weight data (analog) is gathered. In addition, the status of the valve (open/shut) and the conveyor (moving or stationary) would probably be signalled as single digits, although these might be *represented* by high or low voltages.

(*b*) The satellite might be corrected by sending signals to point the rocket motor in a certain direction and to switch it on and to switch it off after a certain time. The orientation data would require conversion (D-to-A) so as to control servo motors. The on/off signals might remain (logically) digital, although amplifying circuitry might be needed to supply enough voltage to operate the switches on the spacecraft.

The same applies to the weighing process; the control signals would be simple on/off commands (start/stop, open/shut) i.e. digital output.

? **Q 20.11** The 'fantail' patented by Edmund Lee in 1745 was a small wheel with wooden vanes, fitted to the back of the mill with its axis at right angles to that of the main sails (Fig. 20.3 overleaf). This device could automatically rotate the cap of the mill, or (in the case of the post mill) the entire structure of the mill.

? **Q 20.12** The windmill in Fig. 20.7 in the students' text is a *vertical* axis wind turbine; therefore it can accept wind from any direction. Turning it into the wind is meaningless.

? **Q 20.13** If a manufacturer can sell products first and then make them, no money and space need be wasted in keeping the finished goods in stock. Manufacturers of, say, small consumer goods have to produce for stock, whereas car makers are increasingly (thanks to automation) able to manufacture after a customer has made a firm order.

Any recession in the motor industry tends to cause stockpiling in the hope of sales later. Builders of ships and oil rigs hardly ever dare to make a vessel except to order because the investment is too great to risk being unable to sell. They may also be *designed* to order.

? **Q 20.14** All forthcoming requirements for components must be stored so that future stock levels (and shortages) can be anticipated. Outstanding orders must be accounted for so as to avoid *over-ordering* of components which should be on their way.

? **Q 20.15** Optical character recognition (OCR) would be possible for AGVs and would be considerably 'people-friendlier'. Several manufacturers are already testing OCR in this area.

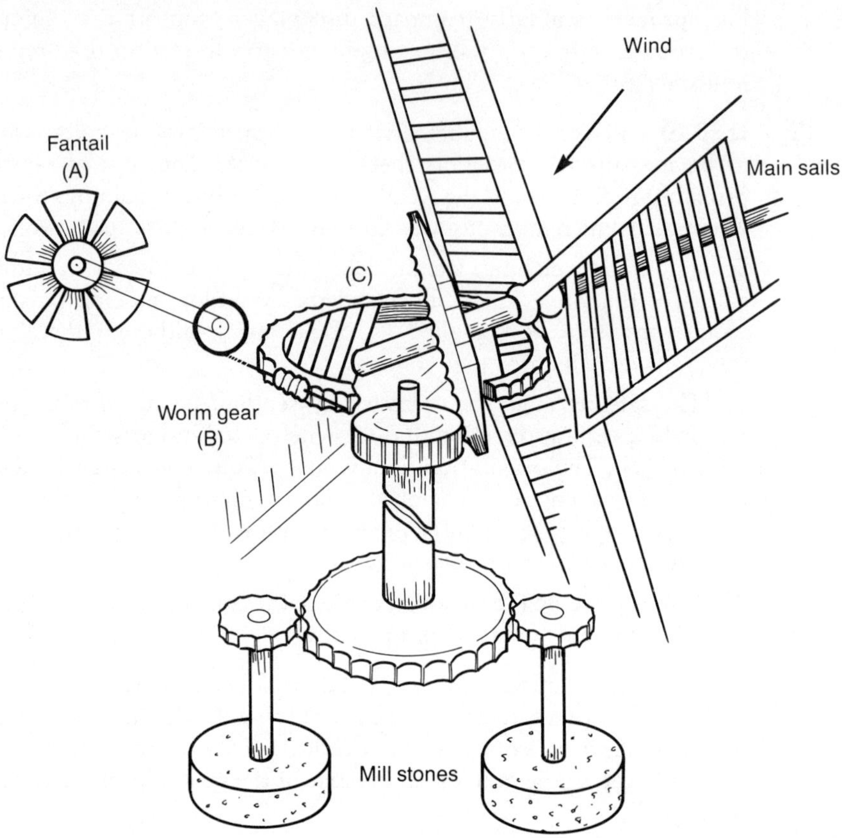

Fig. 20.3 Automatic control of the direction faced by a windmill. Any change in wind direction causes the fantail (A) to start spinning (in either direction depending on the wind shift. This motion is transmitted via gears (B) to the large wooden wheel (C) on which the entire machinery of the mill revolves. The process continues until the main sails are again facing the wind.

? **Q 20.16** *Benefits*: Team spirit, motivation, better quality due to pride in 'their' finished vehicle which is impossible if you are, say, just fitting steering wheels all day.

Drawbacks: Possible loss of the assembly line benefits of productivity through division of labour and rigid scheduling of every small assembly operation.

? **Q 20.17** In the authors' view, the three key reasons in *probable* order of importance, are:

(i) complacent, short-sighted or ignorant management
(ii) obstruction from trades unions fearing job losses
(iii) conventional financial wisdom requiring unrealistically short 'payback' periods on capital investments.

Control Exercise: Automated Guided Vehicles

Briefing: Split your class into teams of two, three or four. Using a floor turtle (if available) or a screen turtle, teams should carry out the following tasks:

(*a*) Draw regular polygons (start with a square) with a given number and length of sides.

(*b*) (For more mathematically able groups only) Draw regular polygons with a given number of sides and a given *area*.

(*c*) Follow a particular path (which you can vary) around an imaginary factory floor (such as that in Fig. 20.4, which you can photocopy and distribute).

(*d*) (Harder) Go to any *two* specified bin locations on a warehouse floor (such as that in Fig 20.5, which may be reproduced) and return to the starting position.

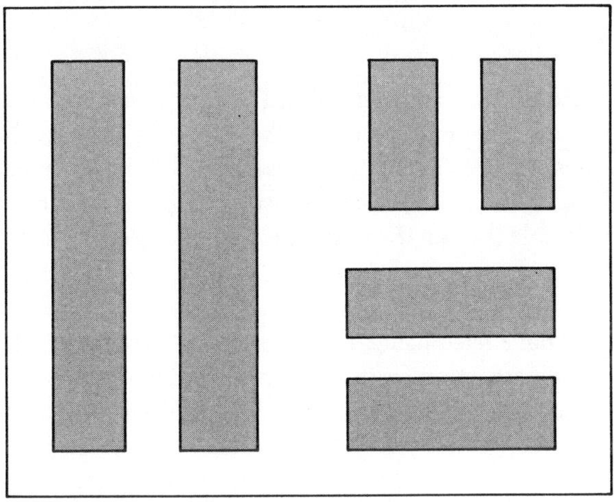

Fig. 20.4 Schematic diagram of a factory floor.

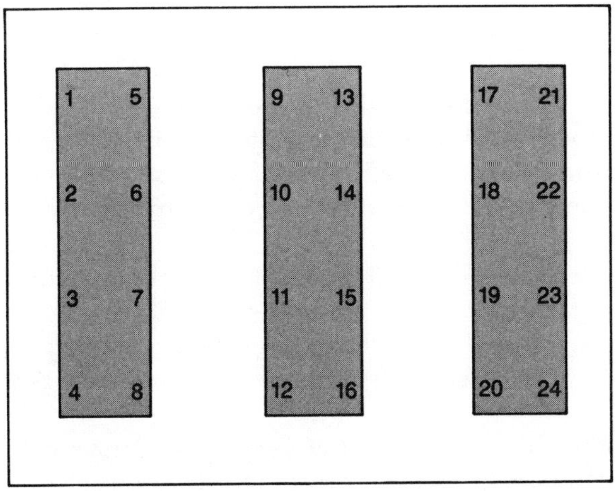

Fig. 20.5 Schematic diagram of a warehouse floor, showing bin locations (in a real warehouse there would be *thousands* of bin locations.)

Do not let any team near a computer or a turtle until you are satisfied that they have analysed the problem, designed and programmed a solution.

Possible division of labour: One team member designs the algorithm to solve each problem, a second codes the solution and a third tests the results. (For tasks 3 and 4, the environment must first be drawn, on floor or screen.) These roles can be switched for subsequent problems.

? **Q 20.18** The research into robots which could replicate themselves is, as mentioned, totally serious, although practical application is clearly some time away. A favourite question of science fiction writers is whether man would always be able to stay 'in control' of the robots, especially as their intelligence advances. We leave teachers and students to discuss, if they wish, the merits of future remote robot colonies.

Most schools and colleges should have a version of LOGO even if they are not fortunate enough to own wheeled floor turtles; these and many other examples can be completed on screen. We have avoided control exercises requiring specific hardware (sensors, stepper motors, buggies, robot arms etc.) valuable though these are, because many schools may not have any such hardware.

You may have tried using 'human robots', 'programmed' to obey unquestioningly any instruction from a volunteer 'controller' (e.g. program David to get up, go and touch the wall, come back and sit down again). This is a most effective way of introducing programming to begin with, particularly to demonstrate the stupid obedience of the computer (students may not be told to stop at the wall or to turn round before sitting down again etc.). It can also help in demonstrating basic control concepts (e.g. David has to sense when he has reached the wall if he is to avoid crashing into it).

If you have a floor turtle the problems with 'blind control' that we have described can be easily demonstrated. For instance, repeat task (*c*) 100 times or so and measure how far the turtle has strayed from its original position. Any divergence would obviously cause trouble in a factory or warehouse.

The most ambitious and able students, if they are fortunate enough to have access to control modules *and* bar-code readers, might attempt to build their own 'smart' AGV, which could get occasional 'fixes' on its position from suitably placed bar codes (like the AGV in Fig. 20.11 in the students' text).

Another, simpler, method of keeping on course is by following light or reflective tracks on the floor. The turtle or other vehicle must be equipped with a sensor, e.g. a light dependent resistor (LDR), to tell when it is heading off track.

21 Serving The Public

The three areas we have chosen to illustrate computer serving the public are important and extensive. Weather forecasting shows computers being used in their first classic role: as super number crunchers. The use by the Police illustrates a varied and important area in which computers have significantly altered what is possible while at the same time raising controversial social issues. In medicine too, computers have significantly altered what is possible and open up a discussion on 'expert systems' in a setting that should be familiar to the students.

All three applications have the same pedagogic consideration in common: they are extensive applications about which students claiming a qualification in GCSE Computer Studies ought to have some knowledge. However they are also specialist areas difficult to present to any depth without 'losing' an audience of teenagers. We hope we have struck the right balance.

Our theme 'Computers serving the public' allows the option of covering all three areas together. Alternatively, since each part is completely independent of the others, you may prefer to deal with each as a separate topic.

DISCUSSION POINTS

Forecasting the Weather

? **Q 21.1** The list is considerable. We have given a good number in the main text: air and shipping lines, farmers and fishermen, building and tourist trades, North Sea oil companies and armed forces. Students will probably think of some more.

? **Q 21.2** Weather information is collected from a number of Met Office ground stations around Britain, from weather balloons launched by the Met Office specifically for that purpose, from coastguard stations on the coast and from oil rigs, lighthouses and ships at sea, from aircraft in flight, and from satellites in space. Furthermore the UK Met Office swaps all its information with other national weather services all around the world.

Q 21.3 Forecasting the weather is difficult because there are so many variables and local variations. To be as accurate as possible, weather analysis needs to be global, for the weather in any one part of the world necessarily depends on developments elsewhere.

Bracknell is one of two World Weather Centres; the other is in Washington, DC. At present only these two weather centres have adequate computing resources to give them operational capability for accurate global analysis.

British weather is particularly complicated, for we are susceptible to so many countervailing influences: the European land mass on the one hand, the Atlantic Ocean on the other; the warmth of the Mediterranean region and the cold of the Arctic.

Some other parts of the world are considerably more settled. To give an extreme example, your authors are confidently predicting that tomorrow the Sahara will be 'hot and dry'. (However, the acid test for a weather man working on more settled regions of the world is his ability to forecast a change however frequent or infrequent that may be.)

Q 21.4 The Met Office claims an accuracy of around 85% for their 24-hour daily forecast for Britain. Their forecasts are improving and their three-day forecasts are now regularly more accurate than the one-day forecasts made ten years ago.

Q 21.5 Validating. The data is being checked by appropriate software routines to establish its acceptability.

Q 21.6 Optical character recognition (see Chapter 5).

Q 21.7 Weather information is stored for:

(i) historical analysis of weather patterns which often provides valuable clues to the physical processes that control the evolution of the weather over long periods.

Thus a long-term prediction might be based on reasoning such as 'when this atmospheric pattern last developed in 1967, such and such followed because the Atlantic was warmer than usual for this time of year'.

(ii) research into weather systems; being able to compare the actual weather with the weather variables before and after allows researchers to extend their knowledge of how the weather behaves.

Q 21.8 If the main processor at Bracknell fails then its main users, such as the airlines, will automatically turn to output from the American World Weather Station in Washington. In the same way, if the American equipment should fail, its users will automatically switch to output from Bracknell. The chance of both systems failing simultaneously is extremely remote.

(Bracknell and Washington and other major weather forecasting agencies around the world are in constant communication anyhow, continually swapping data and forecasts. Reciprocal 'emergency processing' arrangements are the norm in many computing applications.)

? **Q 21.9** The Met Office (naturally) claims that its forecasts are more accurate than anyone else's, including the Americans'. 75% of the world's airlines use Bracknell's weather predictions for flight planning.

However the professionals themselves are the first to agree that forecasts made in sufficient detail and within a time span short enough to be of much use will probably *never* achieve 100% accuracy.

The problems of weather forecasting are formidable and will tax the best scientific brains for many years to come. Nevertheless the forecasts are improving and perhaps 95% accuracy will be obtainable.

As communications networks and satellite information increase in sophistication, so too will the weather forecasters' mathematical equations simulating the atmosphere. Solving these ever more complex equations will depend critically on simultaneous improvement in the computing power available.

? **Q 21.10** The month-in-advance 'long-range' forecasts were never particularly successful: the predictions for several weeks ahead were too often wrong and so the Met Office has stopped broadcasting them to the public.

However the Met Office still does make them, but only for its own research purposes and 'to order' for organisations needing such forecasts for specific purposes where they have proved to be useful.

? **Q 21.11** Yes. The estimated value of the Met Office to the UK economy is some £500 million per year. The weather predictions are crucial to many serious users; the TV and radio forecasts are a minor aspect of the Met Office's business.

(In fact in 1985 the Met Office installed a new IBM 3081 and so the level of public investment in the weather service in recent years has been considerable.)

? **Q 21.12** The routine administration procedures of the Met Office, such as payroll, word processing and so on, are also computerised.

Computers in the Police Service

? **Q 21.13** Real-time systems receive data continuously from outside sources and process it sufficiently rapidly to influence the source.

Police software does not work in real time since it is not part of a process control system.

? **Q 21.14** A high proportion of police work is on 'life or death' emergencies and the collapse of the police computer network is too dangerous to contemplate.

? **Q 21.15** See Chapter 11. Physical restrictions are stringent, e.g. in one of their hand-outs, the police describe the building housing the PNC complex as like a small fortress'. Constant checks are made to see who is using the computer and, of course, police software prevents access to those who do not know the correct codes. So even authorised users of the PNC such as the regular police cannot access parts of some files, e.g. those used by Special Branch.

There is also now a special subsection of the Fraud Squad, operating from Scotland Yard, specialising in investigation of computer fraud.

? **Q 21.16** Although, historically, organisation of the police has been a local responsibility, crime is often a national enterprise and close co-operation between the local forces is obviously of prime importance. If they all ran completely incompatible computer systems then inter-force liaison would be severely hampered.

Whether or not we want or need a national police force is a separate matter and one of some current political controversy.

? **Q 21.17** Students will probably suggest that the hardware needs to be standardised. In fact it need not, as long as it is possible to interface the local system with the national network.

It is more important that the software is completely compatible so that files of information may be exchanged and processed both nationally and/or on the local computer, and that forms, operational procedures and screen displays are the same so that personnel can operate equipment comfortably and efficiently in different locations.

If a computer is designed entirely for some local purpose (e.g. the 999 emergency system described in the text) and to be operated entirely by a specialist team of local officers, then compatibility with some Home Office standard is not particularly important.

However, there may be cost implications if each force operates an independent purchasing policy. Interfacing systems can be complex and expensive.

? **Q 21.18** Good policemen 'know the community'. Information for the computer is collected from the 'bobby pounding the beat'.

Of course this information will not be available to colleagues or other forces *unless* the policeman reports his knowledge to the computer system!

? **Q 21.19** The system described is that of the Metropolitan Police. When it was set up in 1982 it was thought that linking private numbers with private addresses would be too great an invasion of personal privacy.

Students may suggest 'file space'. This is *not* the reason. In any case, it would not be hard to store even the four volumes of the London telephone directory on disk.

? **Q 21.20** If the caller gives the telephone number, the computer can check the three-digit exchange code. Thus SE20 numbers begin 01-659 . . . and SE25 numbers begin 01-653 . . .

? **Q 21.21** Because, apart from local 'joy riders', most car thieves will drive a stolen vehicle out of the area immediately after stealing it.

? **Q 21.22** Tracking stolen cars quickly is important to the police because stolen cars are so often used to stage more elaborate and dangerous crimes.

? **Q 21.23** See Fig. 21.13 in the students' text. A manual system would be too slow and cumbersome and would make the routine check on the ownership of any speeding or badly driven car impractical.

? **Q 21.24** The authors know of two such past experiments: one on the M1 just outside London (North of junction 9 at Flamstead) and the other by the Dartford Tunnel (where traffic slows down for the tolls). Other countries, e.g. Japan, are making extensive use of this technology.

Obviously, knowing that a stolen vehicle has just joined the motorway and is heading in a particular direction makes it possible for the police to intercept it and make an arrest.

The existence of these machines, however, is a matter of concern for they also make it possible for the police to monitor (and possibly intercept) the travelling public for other, possibly political, reasons.

? **Q 21.25–21.29** The whole issue of police computers versus civil liberties is an extremely delicate one.

It is the age-old issue of the state versus the individual—the very stuff of politics—in a context that is both modern and practical.

For our part we have tried to put both sides of the case and ask questions that might provoke students into thinking through the issues for themselves.

Incidentally, Merseyside Police were virtually told by their Police Committee (the council committee that oversees their operation) that they could not be trusted with the computer power they were requesting. Our suggested scenario is a realistic one.

With the right class you might organise a debate as a mock council debate with two parties—the Pros and Antis—taking a series of contributions from those who feel strongest on both sides and a vote at the end.

Computers in the National Health Service

? **Q 21.32** Obviously the first requirement is the computer itself. The size and power of the machine required will depend on the size of the hospital and the details of the records they intend to keep.

In addition the hospital would need reliable hard disk storage, with appropriate back-up (probably a second disk system) and VDU terminals at the reception/appointments desk as well as a printer (of at least near-letter quality) to print out appointment cards and registration details.

Since the system planned will only handle 'registration and appointments' (as specified in the question) the hospital should not need much more than this.

? **Q 21.33** By April 1987, all hospital computer systems were required to conform to NHS guidelines. If ultimately computer records are to be exchanged swiftly and readily between various medical institutions, i.e. local GPs' surgeries, various clinics, different general hospitals and specialist consultancies, it is imperative that computer practices are standardised.

? **Q 21.34** If the system is to be extended so that patients' medical notes are to be recorded as well then the system may require significant expansion.

There will have to be an extensive network of terminals, i.e. a local area network or LAN, serving the medical staff throughout the hospital.

The level of computing power (the network will be complicated to run) and storage space required (medical records are likely to be lengthy) will need to be very considerably increased. The medical staff will also need to be able to print out medical records at work stations conveniently placed.

So although the principle of computerised administrative records for each individual patient is a considerable step towards computerised medical records, the move cannot be made without considerable investment in hardware.

Dramatic advances in optical storage methods are altering the position as we write. A machine-readable 'laser card', the size of a credit card, can now store several megabytes. Medical records will probably be one of the first applications of these cards.

? **Q 21.35** Of the large number of patients that a doctor has on his or her books at any time, some will be seeking advice for emotional, psychiatric or sexual reasons and others will be in the various stages of ailments that the doctor fears will prove terminal (the patient does not always know this). Even those of us with routine uninteresting ailments mostly do not want others to know more than we choose to tell them.

Confidentiality of medical records is an important tradition of the medical profession and a doctor will normally only reveal the records of the patient in his care if the patient has consented or if the police have persuaded a judge (*not* just a local magistrate) to grant them special permission.

As the administrative officers will share the same network as the medical staff, it will be necessary to block access to part of the patients' records for those terminals used in the non-medical sections of the hospital. Furthermore, the doctors can be required to use passcodes to access the medical files.

? **Q 21.36** We have set this here because there are enough pointers in the text for students, at this stage in the course, to make a good job of answering for themselves what is essentially a standard examination question.

(*a*) The computer system will enable the doctors to maintain and update the 8500 records more easily than at present with the manual system. Retrieval of information should be faster and more flexible when not requiring the use of cards and a card index system.

(*b*) The hardware required would depend on the number of users (presumably, four: the three doctors and the receptionist) the number of records to be held (8500) and the level of detail required (each record presumably carries fairly detailed information).

The doctor's system could be well serviced by one of the better quality business microcomputer systems now on the market with a built in hard Winchester disk, which can now be obtained at reasonable cost. (Floppy disks probably could not cope because of the volume of information to be recorded, although they might suffice for a smaller practice.) Information recorded on the disks should be backed up by tape or by a second disk system (with removable cartridges so that the back-up disks may be taken from the premises and stored in a safe place each evening).

A good quality printer, of at least near-letter quality, would also be essential for printing prescriptions, notes to other doctors (such as those working in the local hospitals) and appointments.

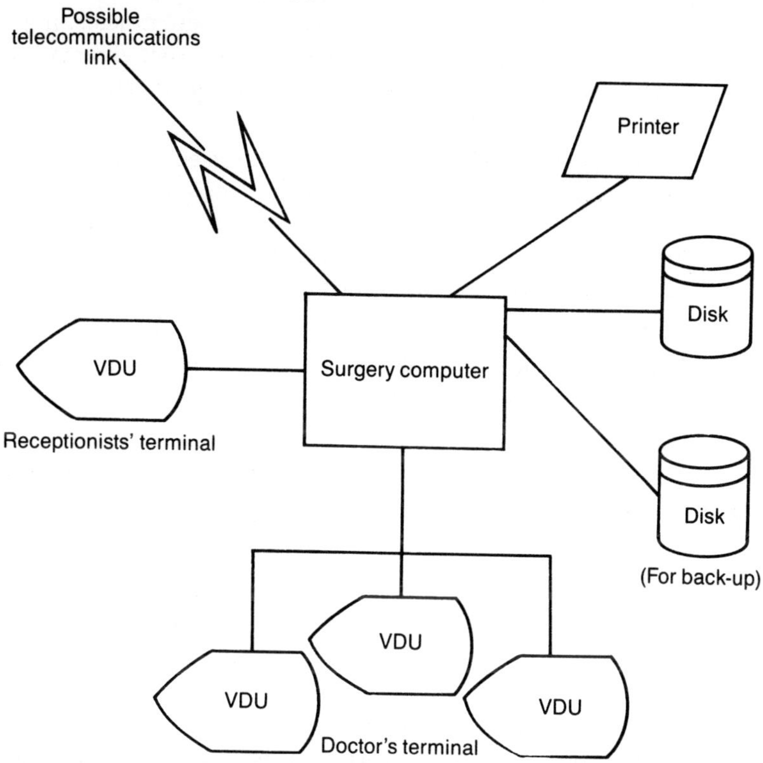

Fig. 21.1 Systems flowchart for the surgery

Such a system should ensure that the doctor has all the required speed of access, processing power, reliability and security.

It could be extended too, so that each doctor could have a terminal at home, connecting to the surgery computer as required through the telephone system and a modem. This would offer the doctor 'on call' the possibility of checking a record from home before making a night call on a patient.

(*c*) The doctors should look for an appropriate software package (there are several to choose from) already running in another surgery.

(*d*) The patients' files might include NHS number, name, address, telephone number, sex, date of birth, occupation, doctor (this is a joint practice of three doctors), next of kin, date of last visit, brief medical history including details of the drugs prescribed with dates, and the date of the patient's last visit. This is not necessarily an exhaustive list; the doctors may wish to include other details and students may have some good suggestions.

(*e*) A patient with a chronic ailment might have a prescription flagged in some way so that the prescription could be issued automatically on request; obviously the system would record every issue of the prescription (the doctor needs to sign it anyway and so the system could never be totally automatic) and be programmed to indicate any unacceptably frequent use of the drug.

(*f*) The computer offers many ways of improving the service that GPs offer their patients. Better kept records are likely in themselves to lead to better treatment. More efficient organisation of appointments, improved facilities for repeat prescriptions and reminder notices sent automatically if a patient is due for a routine check-up should mean greater convenience for the patients.

It may also be possible to build into the system some 'expert' advice so that a doctor about to prescribe drug X which would be incompatible with another drug Y that the patient is already taking is warned by the computer. Alternatively every suggested prescription may bring up on screen a list of possible side effects. In ways such as these the medical service itself might be improved.

? **Q 21.37** OMR is a cheap and simple way of indicating alternatives (as in a multiple choice exam). It is also fast and accurate.

The computer reads the menu cards in batches and so the operator need only type in the ward name once at the beginning of each new batch.

? **Q 21.38** Stock levels could be controlled in ways similar to those described for supermarkets in Chapter 15.

The pharmacist would need to key into the computer the drug code, the code for the doctor to whom the drug was issued, and the quantity taken.

The computer could keep a running total of the quantities of each drug issued to each doctor over a preprogrammed period, say six months, and highlight any abnormally high issues. Of course, a higher than average use of a drug does not prove that a doctor is misusing it, but if he were this would be the first step in the pharmacist's finding out.

? **Q 21.39** This is only true when the patients can input the data themselves. It seems that people are more likely to reveal certain details of their illnesses or life styles to a machine which will not show disapproval. So excessive drinking or drug taking, for example, which could well have a bearing upon many illnesses, are more likely to come to light at an early stage in the diagnostic procedure.

? **Q 21.40** Many GPs will probably welcome such an important medical advance. Many of them are hard pressed and unable to give their patients the time and attention they would like; a computerised medical expert system may considerably help to reduce the pressures.

Some GPs may resent the automation of their professional skill and see the computer systems as a threat to their livelihood.

Q 21.41 Other professional advisory services, e.g. the law and financial services such as accounting or insurance/mortgage brokerage, may find their services computerised in a similar way.

22 Changing Society

The authors have tried to be impartial in this book, but discussing the impact of technology on society is virtually impossible without expressing some personal opinions. We are optimists, although we believe that 'full employment' in the traditional sense will never return. We see the danger of society polarising into 'two nations' as very real, yet we perceive the redefinition of work as a major opportunity rather than a disaster. These views are of course open to question.

DISCUSSION POINTS

Q 22.1 An historical perspective is a great help to understanding how technology is affecting life *today*, but the impact of the Industrial Revolution is still the subject of vehement debate.

(*a*) T. S. Ashton: 'The Industrial Revolution 1760–1830' (Oxford University Press) is an excellent brief survey of the period. For a favourable view on the impact on the workers see R. M. Hartwell: 'The rising standard of living in England, 1800–1850', *Economic History Review*, April 1961; for the pessimistic, alternative view see E. J. Hobsbawm: 'The British standard of living, 1790–1850', *Economic History Review*, August 1957.

(*b*) (i) and (ii) James Hargreaves (died 1778) was an English weaver and carpenter who lived near Blackburn, Lancashire. Around 1764 he invented the spinning jenny (named after his daughter) with which several threads could be spun simultaneously. Local spinners, who feared that the jenny would threaten their jobs, broke into his home and smashed his machines.

He moved to Nottingham, where he set up a small mill and continued to manufacture yarn until his death.

(iii) Joseph-Marie Jacquard (1752–1834) was the French inventor of the Jacquard loom, completed around 1801. It was the first device to use punched cards to control a process, weaving figured patterns according to the holes punched. With this device, any worker could weave complex and beautiful designs which previously took great skill and a long time to produce. The principle was later adopted by Babbage. Although Napoleon gave Jacquard a pension and the Légion d'Honneur, he was extremely unpopular with silk weavers, who threatened his life.

(iv) The Luddites were a group of Nottingham frameworkers, supposedly named after their leader, Ned Ludd (Ludd may not have existed). They destroyed labour-saving machinery (1811–13), fearing that their livelihoods were at risk. Luddism spread to other cities but was severely repressed.

? **Q 22.3** Possible 'entry points' for trainees into a data processing department are shown on the bottom row of Fig. 22.2 in the students' text. Further comments on careers in computing are on pages 131–35 of this Teacher's Guide.

? **Q 22.4** (*a*) In 1800, it was normal for most occupations to work from dawn until dusk, with short breakfast and dinner breaks. However, many employers were by then introducing artificial lighting, using coal-gas, which enabled factories to work day and night. Working days of 14 hours or more were not uncommon; there is at least one documented case of an 18-hour day.

(*b*) In 1900, a ten-hour working day was typical.

? **Q 22.6** It should be strongly emphasised that computer skills are an *addition* to, not a substitute for, basic literacy and numeracy. Language is, and will remain, the most vital tool possessed by mankind, not just for learning but for every aspect of life.

Equally, *everyone* should achieve numeracy; *all* occupations and pursuits require it.

Useful devices like spelling-checkers, spreadsheet programs and even pocket calculators can break down; we should beware of becoming too dependent on the technology.

? **Q 22.7** There are of course a number of non-financial aspects to employment, for example: security, variety of activity, the sense of direction given by specific goals, the scope for decision taking, development of skills and knowledge, interpersonal contact, status and self-esteem.

These are among the rewards that people enjoy, to differing degrees, from jobs. Conversely, unemployment may cause the loss of any or all of these rewards. When these are combined with the financial losses, the psychological impact can be great.

[?] **Q 22.8** Some economists and politicians propose such a course, advocating a high-employment, low-technology, low-productivity economy. They argue that by keeping existing production methods (or introducing new technology only where the effect on employment is minimal) higher employment could be maintained. More productive foreign competitors are kept at bay by high taxes on imports.

It is our view that such a 'siege economy' would be a disastrous course. The world economy is sustained by international trade, on which smaller countries are especially reliant. In the UK there are terrible lessons to be learned from experience. The once-great cotton industry innovated too little, too late in this century. The tide of imports was temporarily stemmed by high import duties, but essential world markets had been lost; the industry collapsed.

[?] **Q 22.9** One reason is that they receive no feedback, particularly of the sounds which they make. Students may have noticed a related phenomenon when someone who is listening to music through headphones tries to sing along with it. Even if they can *normally* sing in tune, if they cannot hear their own voice they cannot hit the right notes, and the result sounds awful!

[?] **Q 22.10** (*a*) Input is by optical character recognition (OCR). Output is by speech synthesis.

(*b*) Most OCR systems recognise only a limited range of typefaces; few machines can cope with the wide range of styles and sizes which book publishers use. Some OCR readers can read typescript, others cannot. Coloured, dirty or dog-eared pages may be illegible. Until recently all OCR readers were expensive but some cheaper devices are now on the market.

The main drawback of synthesised speech is that it can sound terrible. More recent systems have dramatically improved the quality of sound; it is less 'machine-like' and stored dictionaries enable stresses to be placed on the correct syllables. Much progress has also been made towards building in 'understanding' of syntax and context, which is making whole sentences sound more natural.

In libraries or other public places, of course, headphones are necessary to avoid disturbing others.

(*c*) The processing might include something like:

Finding spaces to see where each word begins and ends.

Converting capital letters to lower case (e.g. at beginning of sentences and proper names).

Looking each word up in a stored dictionary to see which sound units (phonemes) it comprises.

If possible some examination of context for ambiguous cases (e.g. 'lead' 'lead, kindly light' and 'lead' as in 'lead pencil').

Examine punctuation to determine pauses (short pause for a comma and longer pause for a full stop etc.).

Even this detailed processing would not permit output of very realistic speech; even more analysis (see (*b*) above) could improve the results.

? **Q 22.11** (*a*) Electronic mail presents no problems for deaf people, provided they have a computer with a modem and suitable software. British Telecom Gold gives discounts to deaf users.

(*b*) Electronic mail is equally useful for blind people but they need an additional gadget such as the Versabraille in order to read their messages.

? **Q 22.12** Many classes will find this a difficult topic to discuss but we feel that students should be aware of the issues involved.

In our view the progress that has been made in a few years by applying microtechnology to help the disabled and handicapped exceeds the progress made, for instance, in applying it to manufacturing systems over decades.

Computer technology, here as in any field, is not a universal panacea. Many of the problems faced by the disabled or otherwise handicapped remain intractable. However, computers have opened up hitherto unimagined possibilities for thousands of people.

There is such a variety of devices in use that we have only provided a glimpse of the vast range. Health authorities and/or Social Services departments may supply information and aids. LEAs normally have specialists who can advise on available aids for educational purposes. Some addresses are given on pages 136–41 of this Guide.

If your class does come up with any ideas for software or hardware devices that could be of value and which they are keen to explore, several points should be remembered.

(i) Encourage them to set clear objectives; what is it intended to do and how will it do it?
(ii) Who exactly is going to use it?
(iii) Is there a simpler way to solve the problem?
(iv) Has it already been invented? Nothing is more frustrating than spending a great deal of time devising something that already exists.
(v) Get professional advice, both to check (iv) and to establish the basic feasibility of the idea, otherwise major errors are likely.
(vi) Make sure that any prototype is robust. If it involves software is it 'crashproof'? If it is hardware can anyone use it, or is it too fragile? Is it safe?

? **Q 22.13** (*a*) The Data Protection Act should reduce the misuse of personal data, although it has been criticised for not going further. The 'data subject', i.e. person about whom data is stored, has the right to be informed whether such data is held, and to inspect it. However, the onus is on the data subject to ask for the information, rather than on the data user to provide it.

The Younger Report on privacy and the Lindop Report proposed a legally binding code of practice for computer users. But the Government stopped short of creating a Data Protection Authority with a more active policing role, and settled for a register of users and their files.

The Registrar does have considerable powers to forbid organisations from processing personal data if he believes the Act is being infringed. However, the maximum penalty on summary conviction is a £1000 fine. The real weakness may be simply lack of staff to deal with as many as 400 000 registrations under the Act.

(*b*) Many observers regard this as a serious weakness. Although the Act covers any information which is recorded in a form in which it *may* be processed on computers, an ordinary card index is outside the scope of the Act. So, too, are quite sophisticated manual record handling systems. These are clearly open to abuse, although bringing them within the scope of the Act would increase the administrative problems even further.

? **Q 22.14** Data held for:

(*a*) The prevention or detection of crime

(*b*) The apprehension or prosecution of offenders

(*c*) The assessment or collection of any tax or duty

is exempt from *subject access* if such access would be likely to prejudice one of those matters. It remains subject to the other Data Protection Principles, which require that the data is obtained and processed fairly and lawfully, is kept only for specified and lawful purposes, is accurate, up to date, adequate, relevant and not excessive, and is kept no longer than necessary.

Police work would of course be impossible if the exemption from subject access did not apply. It is too soon to say whether the Act is an adequate safeguard against violation of the other Data Protection principles.

? **Q 22.15** (*a*) Identity badges for football supporters would be unlikely to infringe anyone's rights. Anyone who objected would be at liberty not to attend football matches. The card required in order to gain access to a football ground would not be different in principle from a membership card for any other club (e.g. a nightclub, the AA or the RAC). Whether it would help to reduce hooliganism is another question.

(*b*) Identity documents for all citizens would be more controversial, as they could not be avoided. See also Q 5.19 and Q 5.20.

Part E Inside the CPU

23 Data Representation

Inevitably, this chapter is considerably more mathematical than the rest of the book. We do not envisage it being taught in quite the same way. Most students will benefit from a classroom discussion of the principles before they attempt the chapter, rather than the other way round.

We have tried to keep the concepts as simple as possible while nevertheless covering the content of the GCSE syllabuses; all the Examining Groups seem to require much the same level of understanding, namely an appreciation of the ideas and no more, although not all require an appreciation of binary fractions.

DISCUSSION POINTS

? **Q 23.3** (*a*) $2^6 = 64$ (*b*) $2^7 = 128$ (*c*)$2^8 = 256$

? **Q 23.4** 36. No, a 5-bit byte can carry only 32 unique codes which is not enough for even the most basic character set of 36 symbols. (But in any case a computer could not manage with just these 36 symbols; additional codes for punctuation, arithmetic symbols and control codes are necessary.)

It follows that any computer must use at least a 6-bit byte if it is to code the symbols human beings will want to use. The early computers were 6-bit byte machines (and as a consequence the early languages assumed only a set of capital letters). However the 64 options available using a 6-bit byte are only just enough and greatly restrict the possible use of graphics and elaborate control functions.

? **Q 23.5** 85. This is too many for even a 6-bit byte (which allows 64 unique codes). Seven bits would suffice, but modern computers also carry an eighth parity bit.

Q 23.6 The parity bits serve as a check when transmitting output, whether to the computer screen a few centimetres away or over hundreds of kilometres to some remote location. In practice many microcomputers do not use a parity bit internally and so the 8th bit is used to indicate an alternative character set (e.g. italics or graphics characters).

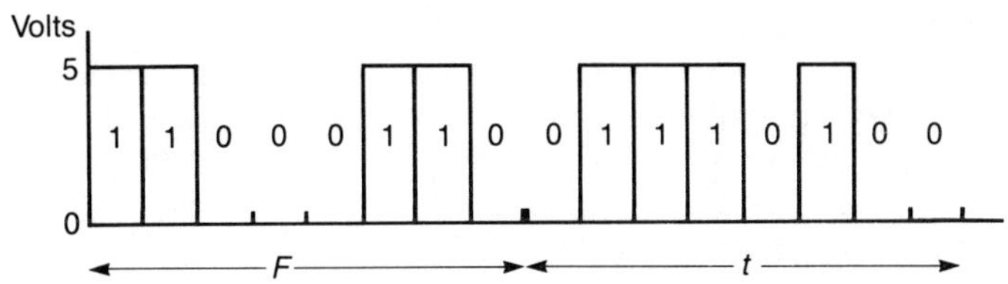

Fig. 23.1 The electronic pulse stream for the character string 'Ft'

Q 23.7 (*a*) 11 (*b*) 29 (*c*) 41 (*d*) 238
(*e*) 199 (*f*) 117 (*g*) 166 (*h*) 255

Q 23.8 (*a*) 0000 1001 (*b*) 0000 1101
(*c*) 0001 1100 (*d*) 0101 1001
(*e*) 0110 1001 (*f*) 1001 1011
(*g*) 1110 1000 (*h*) 1111 1111

Q 23.9 01 1000 0011. A 10 digit number does not fit inside an 8-bit byte and so the computer will use two bytes to represent it. The largest number two bytes can represent is $2^{16} - 1 = 65\,535$.

Q 23.11 (*a*) 20 (*b*) 81 (*c*) 26 (*d*) 44 (*e*) 201 (*f*) 190

Q 23.12 (*a*) 11 = 17 (*b*) 36 = 54 (*c*) 8C = 140
(*d*) 46 = 70 (*e*) 98 = 155 (*f*) AF = 175

Q 23.13 (*a*) 16 = 0001 0110 (*b*) 26 = 0010 0110
(*c*) 33 = 0011 0011 (*d*) 3E = 0011 1110
(*e*) AC = 1010 1100 (*f*) F9 = 1111 1001

Q 23.14 (*a*) +7 (*b*) −28 (*c*) −11

Q 23.15 (*a*) 0001 0111 (*b*) 1001 0111
(*c*) 0000 1001 (*d*) 1000 1001
(*e*) 0011 1000 (*f*) 1011 1000
(*g*) 0101 0111 (*h*) 1101 0111

Q 23.16 (*a*) 1111 1101 (*b*) 1111 0101
(*c*) 1111 0100 (*d*) 1111 0001

? **Q 23.18** (*a*) 1001 1101 (*b*) 1100 1101 (*c*) 1000 0001

? **Q 23.19** (*a*) −95 (*b*) −70 (*c*) −38

? **Q 23.21** (*a*) +127 (*b*) −1 (*c*) 0
(*d*) −128; the range is −128 to +127

? **Q 23.22** 9; −9

? **Q 23.23**

```
  0000 1101
  1111 0111
-----------
1 0000 0100 = +4
-----------
↑
lose the
extra
bit
```

(the leading 1 is struck through)

? **Q 23.24**

(*a*)	0000 1001	i.e.	54	− 45	=	9
(*b*)	0001 0111	i.e.	109	− 86	=	23
(*c*)	0010 1010	i.e.	85	− 43	=	42
(*d*)	0000 0111	i.e.	109	− 102	=	7
(*e*)	1101 1011	i.e.	58	− 95	=	−37
(*f*)	1001 0000	i.e.	−95	− 17	=	−112

? **Q 23.25** (*a*) $3\frac{1}{4}$ (*b*) $26\frac{1}{2}$ (*c*) $31\frac{3}{4}$

? **Q 23.26** (*a*) 0000 0101 (*b*) 0000 1010 (*c*) 0010 0101
(*d*) 0011 0011 (*e*) 0000 0001

? **Q 23.27** (*a*) $.1342 \times 10^3$ (*b*) $.4324 \times 10^2$ (*c*) $.16302 \times 10^2$
(*d*) $.22103 \times 10^3$ (*e*) $.12 \times 10^{-1}$ (*f*) $.21 \times 10^{-3}$
(*g*) $.31 \times 10^{-3}$ (*h*) $.23 \times 10^{-4}$

? **Q 23.28** (*a*) $\frac{11}{16} \times 2^1 = 1\frac{3}{8}$ or 1.375 (*b*) $\frac{5}{8} \times 2^2 = 2\frac{1}{2}$ or 2.5
(*c*) $\frac{13}{16} \times 2^3 = 6\frac{1}{2}$ or 6.5 (*d*) $-\frac{11}{16} \times 2^2 = -2\frac{3}{4}$ or −2.75
(*e*) $\frac{7}{8} \times 2^{-3} = \frac{7}{64}$ or 0.109375 (*f*) $\frac{3}{4} \times 2^{-1} = \frac{3}{8}$ or 0.375

? **Q 23.29** $2^{15} - 1 = 32767$
Complement notation will allow −32768 and so the numbers that cannot be represented begin with +32768 and −32769.

? **Q 23.30** Students will probably try to build up the numbers as 0.25 + 0.125 etc. A quicker method is to treat the byte as a multiple of 1/128.

For example 0.1 × 128 = 12.8 which rounds to 13 (to the nearest whole number). So the closest we can get is 13/128 = 0.1015625.

Similarly as 0.3 × 128 = 38.4 ≈ 38, the closest we can get to 0.3 is 38/128 = 0.296875; and the closest to 0.7 is 90/128 = 0.703125.

EXERCISES 23

Q 2 B, C, E

Q 3 (*a*) $2^7 = 128$

Q 5 (*a*) 84 (*b*) n (*c*) Upper and lower case (*d*) COMPILER
(*e*) Punctuation marks, other symbols such as $, £ and #, control and graphics characters.

Q 6 (*a*) 10011011

Q 7 (*c*) −9 = | 1 | 1 | 1 | 1 | 0 | 1 | 1 | 1 |

Q 8 (*c*) (i)

```
  11101
+  1101
-------
 101010
-------
```

(ii) −

```
  101101       101101
-  10101     + 101011
             --------
               011001
             --------
```

(*d*) (i) | 1 | 0 | 0 | 1 | 1 | (ii) −1

Q 9 (*a*) 23 = 00010111
1's complement = 11101000
2's complement = 11101001
(*d*) 46 = 00101110 i.e. 23 shifted one place to the left.

(*e*)

```
  46      00101110
 −23      11101001
         ---------
          00010111
         ---------
         ↑
         lose extra
         bit
```

43 lies outside the range of numbers that may be represented with a 6-bit byte using 2's complements. (The range for such a byte is −32 to +31.)

Q 10

```
 +35      0 0100011
−121    + 1 0000111   (in 2's complement form)
        -----------
          1 0101010
        -----------
```

(There is no extra bit to lose since the answer is negative: −86.)

24 The CPU

In line with the syllabuses of the five GCSE examining groups we have deliberately avoided extensive analysis of the internal workings of the computer. However we have discussed the three main components of the CPU, giving students an idea of their main function and a very simple outline of how they work.

It is our view that, in the past, computer studies courses at O-level and CSE have placed too great an emphasis on logic gates, machine code, assembler and the like, without actually teaching much of real use. The internal working of a computer is, after all, a hugely complex subject much above what could be reasonably expected of even the brightest school students.

Nevertheless it is proper that students expecting to gain a formal qualification in computer studies should have some idea, even if only an elementary one, of what goes on inside the 'black boxes'.

There is also some scope for practical work here:

(*a*) Students should be encouraged to build for themselves simple AND and OR electrical circuits. Explore the logic by asking two students to operate the switches A and B in answer to a pair of simple true/false questions.

(*b*) The fetch-execute cycle could be illustrated by (*a*) six students playing the rôle of (i) the program, (ii) central memory, (iii) the ALU, (iv) the input device, (v) the output device and (vi) the control unit for some simple program, e.g. following a simple algebraic formula such as A * B – C.

DISCUSSION POINTS

? **Q 24.1** Exactly what happens depends on the size of the printer's buffer, (a temporary store) which can vary from zero to many kilobytes. The computer will fill the buffer and await a signal back from the printer that it is ready for further output. Some machines, however, do not automatically check that the printer is free, resulting in lost output.

? **Q 24.2** Non-volatile RAM was discussed in Chapter 7: 'bubble' memory, and battery powered RAM are non-volatile; other devices are under development.

Q 24.3 In the first line of the table, the washing machine is not operating since the control switch W has not been set to wash and the door D is not shut (although the hot water H is on).

In line two the door has been shut, but the control switch is still not set to 'wash'.

Only in the third line are all three conditions true and the wash cycle begins.

This may seem a trivial example but we feel it worth spelling out to students that all computerised control systems work essentially on these principles.

The complete table would be:

W	D	H	Wash cycle
0	0	1	0
0	1	1	0
1	1	1	1
0	0	0	0
0	1	0	0
1	0	0	0
1	0	1	0
1	1	0	0

You might use this opportunity to point out the importance of a systematic order when constructing a truth table. The question has made this difficult here.

Q 24.4

(a)

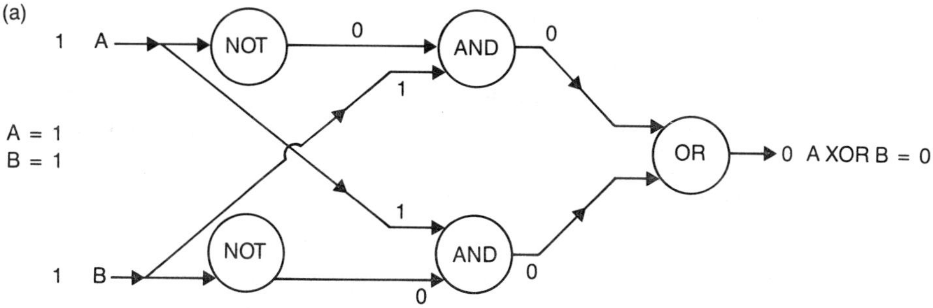

(b)

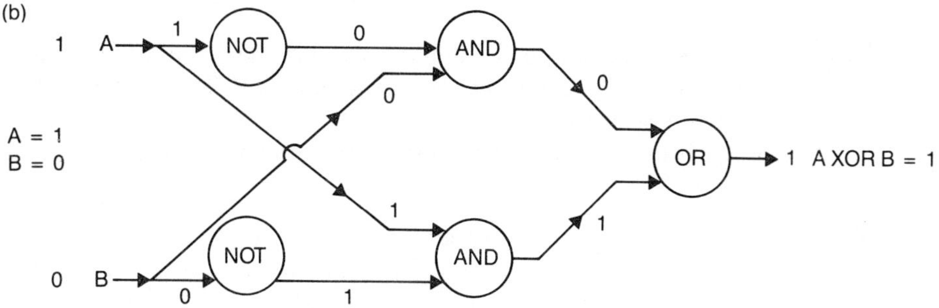

(c)

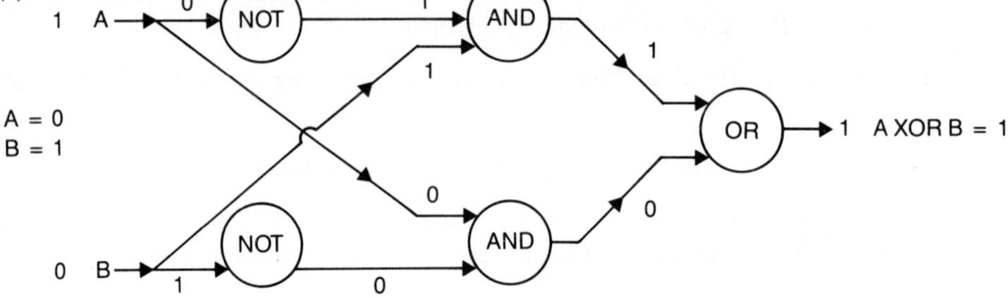

(d)

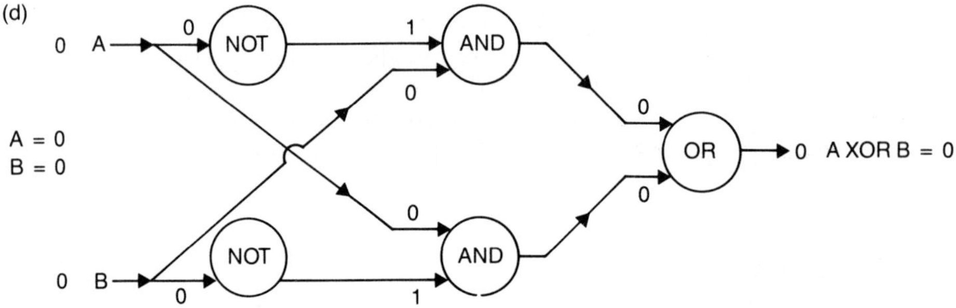

We have used XOR following one or two of the examining groups in preference to EOR (used by BBC BASIC among others).

If you wish to demonstrate the operation of the XOR circuit to the class, you could build a simple electrical circuit using two two-way switches. However these work rather differently from an electronic XOR gate. (The switches are arranged to complete one of two circuits.)

Note that our discussion of logic gates ends here. We have deliberately excluded NAND and NOR gates. You might want to mention these in passing and have the students draw up relevant truth tables, if your class is a good one. However we do not recommend that you extend the treatment any further than that. GCSE simply does not require it.

? **Q 24.5–24.6** The computer automatically puts the first line of program into a predetermined memory location. The command RUN causes the computer to fetch the first instruction from that location, and the fetch-execute cycle begins, each instruction having been stored (and so executed) in sequence.

? **Q 24.7** A large number of BASIC instructions known even to a moderate programmer will cause the program to jump out of simple sequence: GOTO, FOR . . . NEXT, REPEAT . . . UNTIL, IF . . . THEN . . . ELSE . . ., GOSUB, RETURN, PROC, ENDPROC etc. . . .

? **Q 24.9** The program inputs two separate numbers, adds them together, storing the result (in location 102) as well as displaying it on the VDU screen.

? **Q 24.10** $2^4 = 16$

? **Q 24.11** $2^8 = 256$

EXERCISES 24

Q 6 C

Q 7 P = A AND B; Q = A OR B

Q 8 (*b*)

Inputs A	Inputs B	Outputs C	Outputs D
0	0	0	0
0	1	0	1
1	0	0	1
1	1	1	0

This is a simple 'adder' circuit that follows the laws of binary arithmetic:

0 + 0 = 00
0 + 1 = 01
1 + 0 = 01
1 + 1 = 10

Q 9 (*a*)

Hard disk	Floppy disk	Tape unit	VDU	Printer	
1	1	0	1	1	= 27

(*b*) (i) Hard disk off (ii) Printer on

Q 10 (*a*) Alarm switch, S, on; door or window open (D = 0 or W = 0) or movement in the room (M = 1).

(*b*)

Inputs D	Inputs W	Inputs M	Inputs S	Outputs A
0	0	0	0	0
0	0	0	1	1
0	0	1	0	0
0	0	1	1	1
0	1	0	0	0
0	1	0	1	1
0	1	1	0	0
0	1	1	1	1

Inputs D	Inputs W	Inputs M	Inputs S	Outputs A
1	0	0	0	0
1	0	0	1	1
1	0	1	0	0
1	0	1	1	1
1	1	0	0	0
1	1	0	1	0
1	1	1	0	0
1	1	1	1	1

(*c*)

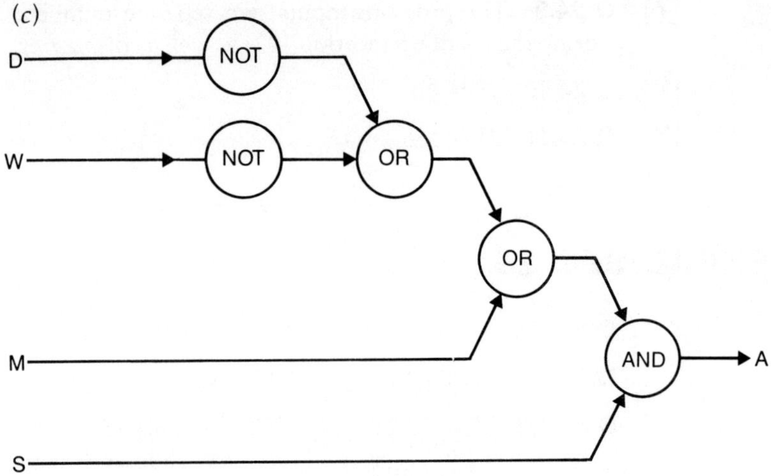

Q 12 (*a*) P machine code; O hexadecimal; R assembly language.
(*b*) 0101 0100
(*c*) 60
(*d*) machine code
(*e*) accumulator
(*f*) assembler or assembly program
(*g*) 010A
(*h*) 0103

Q 13 (*b*) (i) 24
(ii) 6
(iii) ADD 42 (rather than ADD N 42)
(iv) No need to extract contents of location 42.

Evaluating Educational Software

For a detailed analysis of this topic, we highly recommend John Self's book (*Microcomputers in Education, A Critical Appraisal of Educational Software*, Harvester Press, 1985). The best sources of general guidance, and recommendations as to specific software, are, of course, fellow teachers. Their knowledge is invaluable. Your local Teachers' Centre will be able to suggest some user groups or other useful contacts. Otherwise MUSE (see address list on pages 136–41 of this Guide) is a good starting point.

A further recommendation, covering the subject in some depth with specific details about tested programs, is *The Daily Telegraph Guide*, edited by Dr Bill Tagg (see page 145). The following is necessarily a very brief guide to choosing educational software.

First, if at all possible, try before you buy. We suggest seven simple criteria for your initial, rapid appraisal:

1) Will it run on the computer model(s) which you have available?
2) Do you need any extra hardware (peripherals, etc.)? These could be costly, and obviously affect your buying decision.
3) Does it *actually* run? This silly question is, unfortunately, still necessary. Check for yourself.
4) Is it crashproof? Some programs 'hang' for no apparent reason, others crash when you press the wrong key. The test, which professional developers use, is to try everything you can (short of physical damage!) to *make* it crash.
5) Is it easy to use? Remember that your students *might* be more patient than you in working out how to use an inscrutable program, but if it takes too long, or requires too much poring over instruction manuals, it probably will fail in practice.
6) Is it properly presented? This, too, is subjective. We suggest that the packaging and (more importantly) the screen designs should be clear and attractive. Furthermore, spelling mistakes are, we would suggest, unacceptable.
7) Is the accompanying documentation clear, concise and literate?

Any software which passes these tests must then attempt to clear some tougher hurdles, to try to establish its educational value. We suggest seven further criteria; they may help you to evolve your own:

1) Does the software actually help the learning process? If you feel, for example, that reciting the 11 times table does not really help, then it should be obvious that a computer program which gets its user to key in the 11 times table is not going to be any help either. This may sound absurd, but it is remarkable how often critical appraisal is suspended just because one is dealing with a computer program.
2) Does it really use the computer's potential, or would some other method be equally (or more) effective? For instance, the best way for a student to see the result of tossing 12 coins is—wait for it—for the student to take 12 coins, toss them and record the results. But some teachers would have that student gawping at the computer screen instead! Now if you wanted to toss a million coins, the picture is different . . . the computer is of real value to simulate such an experiment.
3) Will the learner be in control of the computer program, or the other way round? To continue the simple example above, can the students *decide* how many coins to toss in each simulated experiment, and compare the results—or must they sit passively through a preset sequence?
4) How flexible is the program? Could the student choose, say, to count heads or tails, to toss groups of coins, to plot histograms or graphs of the results, select screen display or printout—or even, perhaps, to see the effect of 'weighting' the coins?
5) Will it be interesting enough to hold the attention of the learner?
6) Is the program factually accurate? However much scepticism is encouraged in the classroom, some students (if not all) will tend to believe the computer in any event.
7) Is the program really relevant to the subject and/or the curriculum? It is tempting to be seduced by clever, attractive or absorbing programs—which might have very little bearing on the subject under study.

If the program under the spotlight is still looking good, you just might be on to something!

It may be useful to take a quick look at some of the main categories of software used in education:

Drill and Practice

These repetitive question and answer programs may have some limited uses e.g. individual revision, vocabulary testing—but have generally been discredited as a method of effective learning.

Programming Languages

There are dozens of languages available in the education market, which cannot be assessed here. Their potential lies in the immediate access they can give to computing power, and in the creative ways they can encourage learning—by invention and exploration, the most natural ways possible. Seymour Papert may convince the sceptics (see page 86 and pages 142–45).

Information Handling

The ability to manage information is an invaluable skill. Data handling (including word processing) packages can afford tremendous opportunities for painless learning. When the student cannot wait to gather more data for the files, or when *rewriting* an essay becomes an opportunity rather than a punishment—the teacher is winning the battle!

Communications

Communications software can extend the business of manipulating data and text beyond the confines of your school or college. Accessing networks, viewdata systems and other remote data bases can literally and metaphorically widen the students' horizons.

Software can also communicate to help us to exert control over the immediate physical environment. Classes merely reading about control applications will never understand them as deeply as those able to use robots and control other devices.

Adventures

This category of software is enormously popular and can be turned to good educational effect. Escaping all kinds of dragons may be of limited value, but exploring the Amazon or navigating round the Horn can be another matter.

Planning, map-reading, budgetting and teamwork are among the many skills which can be developed while, say, preparing an 'assault on Everest'.

Simulations

Simulations may often be packed with adventure, as many young people know from 'driving' at Indianapolis or 'flying' a fighter. The same young people are pleasantly surprised to discover how exciting it is to 'run' a business; a hotel, a supermarket—or even a country!

Other excellent simulations (see Chapter 20) realistically reproduce complex chemical or even nuclear reactions, allowing students to interact with the simulated process: a genuine aid to understanding.

Such a brief survey cannot do justice to the diversity of educational software available. Remarkably, we are still only at the beginning; the first 'chapter' of educational software has scarcely been written.

Commercial Software

A package need not be labelled 'educational' before it can assist learning. On the contrary, many schools and colleges are finding that standard commercial software: accounts packages, database, spreadsheets, word processing, etc., may provide invaluable teaching tools. Software suppliers frequently offer educational discounts.

Software Copyright

Finally, a few words on copyright are in order. Copying software (except for genuine back-ups) is theft; the Copyright Act has been amended so as to make this absolutely clear.

Do make sure that your classes understand this.

Several large computer users have sacked staff for making unauthorised copies of software.

Software pirates are depressing the quality of software available by depriving the publishers of the revenue necessary for further development.

Careers in Computing

CAREERS ADVICE

Such is the pace of the computer industry that any computing book is outdated almost as soon as it is published. There should be several books and pamphlets on opportunities in computing in your careers library (or, failing that, your local library). These give a useful overview but most of them, we have found, fail to reflect this extraordinary rate of change and the new types of job which are emerging.

The careers specialist at your school or college should be aware of the latest developments in the job market. Bear in mind, however, that he or she must cover the whole spectrum of careers—so any specific knowledge you can glean could be invaluable.

The Opportunities

The computer industry is remarkably volatile; news stories abound of companies soaring to phenomenal success while others crash with no less spectacle into receivership. The chip industry in particular behaves like a barometer and is prone to violent trade cycles. When one of the US giants like Intel lays off staff, there is no shortage of pundits predicting the collapse of the entire information technology business.

We believe that no such collapse will occur. On the contrary, the foundering of some companies whilst a host of others are spawned is a sign of remarkable vitality (the biotechnological industry is another good example). We cannot expand the argument fully here but refer the reader to (for example) Stonier in the suggested reading list (pages 142–45) and to our discussions in Chapters 22 and 25 of the students' text. Information technology is, in our view, so central to the future of all organisations that it will continue to expand (despite fluctuations) well into the next century. It will bring great challenges and enormous opportunities.

Already in the UK well over half the workers in the service sector are 'technology workers'. In most developed countries we now have the apparent paradox of record unemployment levels while the computer press advertises thousands of vacancies every week.

The Skills Shortage

Data processing managers have complained for many years of a shortage of skilled staff; the inflated salaries which some specialists can command bears witness. Yet, in an industry which is still in its adolescence, it is extraordinary how conservative many of those managers are in taking the steps needed to overcome the crisis.

The gap between the skills needed and the skills available is, very gradually, being bridged. This is being achieved in several ways. Firstly, increasing 'computer literacy' in schools and colleges means that younger workers are more likely to have basic computing skills and be willing to acquire more.

Secondly, government-sponsored initiatives (e.g., Youth Training Schemes, the Technical and Vocational Education Initiative, the Information Technology Centres) have already given Information Technology skills to hundreds of thousands of young people.

Thirdly, employers are beginning to take a serious approach to training existing staff. Training expenditure in the UK is still low by international standards, but the critical importance of developing people and their skills is recognised more and more.

Fourthly, the speed of software development is starting to increase, thanks to the use of various 'productivity tools'. Computer people, swift to chide manufacturers for their slow adoption of automation, are the last people to automate their own production process!

These changes will all affect future career opportunities. We will recap the types of job available and then see where the school-leaver may be able to enter the industry.

TYPES OF JOB

The main job functions in computing are described in Chapter 22 of the main text (the role of the systems/business analyst and the programmer were examined in more detail in Chapter 9). We recommend that students review both these chapters before starting any career discussion.

Typical job titles are shown in Fig. 22.2 in the students' text. There are many variations of organisation structure, but the general trend on the development side is away from specialised analysts who do no programming (and vice versa) to versatile analyst/programmers and business analysts.

The dividing line between operations and systems development remains quite firm in large computer installations. This is partly due to physical separation: the computer room itself is kept air-conditioned and secure; it must be kept free of both dust and intruders—a category usually including programmers and analysts!

Nonetheless, it is quite common for operators to re-train as programmers or analysts, and occasionally systems development people move into operations.

Smaller Computer Installations

Smaller sites can rarely afford enough staff to keep rigid specialisation of job functions. At many minicomputer sites, the 'DPM' may investigate, analyse, design *and* program systems—and often run them as well! Arbitrary demarcation between jobs is usually seen as pointless and inefficient.

The impact of the microcomputer has been to emphasise this still further; the job advertisement may say 'operator' or 'programmer', but it usually means 'business/systems analyst/programmer/operator/data controller/user liaison person'!

Entry Points for School-leavers

Many senior managers, realising that a micro could help them to improve their performance, have had a real struggle simply to find their way around a keyboard. Some have given up! Today's school-leaver with keyboard skills, as well as an appreciation of information systems, has an immediate advantage.

Even the smallest business can now afford a computer, but the proprietor often has neither the time nor the skills needed to ensure its effective use. This offers real opportunities for school-leavers but the business managers themselves are only just beginning to recognise the need. Here again, the job (if advertised at all) may be for an 'office junior', 'filing clerk', 'typist', 'trainee book-keeper', 'receptionist' and so on. In reality, this could well mean, say, data entry to computer systems, word processing, updating or organising a mailing list or some other data base, processing accounts, etc.—in other words, the first step into 'real-life' computing.

Medium-sized and large installations will continue to recruit trainees into various roles: data preparation, data control, operations, programming, analysis, user support (see pupil's book pages 399 and 400). The first three of these are normally more likely to be open to school-leavers, most employers preferring to recruit graduates or those with significant work experience as trainees in systems development or user liaison.

Other Jobs

There are often opportunities with computer and peripheral manufacturers. Young people might be recruited in the warehousing/despatch/distribution areas; others are needed for office jobs, e.g. order processing, accounts, secretarial, customer liaison, etc. Some may be trained for production work, others for engineering and maintenance (many independent companies are now specialising in these areas).

Computer manufacturers also need programmers and analysts, as do software houses (which design and sell software products) and systems houses (which build entire systems, usually selling the complete hardware/software combination). Consultancies, computer bureaux and training companies provide further opportunities, though usually for more experienced staff.

All these organisations need salespeople. This work is a very long way from the common perception of the 'foot-in-door', high-pressure world of double glazing and deep freezes. It requires patience, technical knowledge, excellent communications skills, real ability to analyse and understand a customer's needs, and the utmost professionalism. Such a combination of skills is rare: top salespeople reap high rewards.

School-leavers, of course, could not expect to walk into a job selling high-value systems; this may demand years of experience. But there are avenues into selling via, for instance, office-based customer support—or selling lower-value products such as 'consumables': disks, ribbons, computer stationery, etc.

Types of People Needed

One of the most persistent myths about computer people is that they tend to be 'boffins', in a world of their own, relating more successfully to machines than to people. It really should be stressed that most people in computing spend more of their time dealing with people than with machines: 'people skills' are vital for most computing occupations.

The extrovert might be happiest in sales, user support or consultancy, while the introvert, perhaps, beavers away refining a compiler design or tuning a real-time operating system—but there is no such thing as the ideal personality for a computing career.

Another myth which is gradually waning is the notion that you must be a mathematical prodigy for success in computing. You need intelligence certainly, and a capacity for logical thought, but there is no evidence that mathematical prowess *per se* is a better qualification than, say, fluency in French!

Finally, of course, there is *no* computing work where males or females are to be preferred. Women are still having some trouble breaking through to the top levels in the industry, but this in no way reflects lack of ability or aptitude. It is clear, however, that at schools and colleges boys *will* hog the computers *and* expect to use them effectively. The girls will not only allow this to happen, but also seem to expect to be unsuccessful unless the teacher takes steps to stop this happening and to raise their expectations.

Further Training

Many YTS courses include a substantial element of practical computer training. The Information Technology Centres (ITeCs) provide an even wider range of technology skills, but places are far more limited.

Some students will want to go on to A-level and degree courses in computing. Such courses have been criticised in the past for being too theoretical: some employers even discount a Computer Science degree as largely irrelevant for practical computing purposes! There is now, however, a greater diversity of courses, some with a strong 'applied' bias.

We would not accept the simple 'theory bad–practice good' notion at any level of study, although GCSE was a welcome step towards imparting knowledge so that it can be applied—and parallel evolution of the A-level syllabus is likely to follow.

Your careers adviser will give you the up-to-date picture with regard to specific computing qualifications, which are too numerous to list here. Computing is still an industry in which success is perfectly attainable without formal qualifications.

A school-leaver considering *any* job should always ask what training will be received, and beware of employers whose answers are vague. This is especially important in any computing occupation, where skills must be continually updated.

Flexibility

There are many desirable qualities for computing employees, but if we had to single out one as the most crucial, it would be *flexibility*.

Computer people, like any species, must adapt to survive. Working methods are themselves in a state of flux: many jobs are part-time, a small but growing minority of workers are home-based, tens of thousands are self-employed contractors.

Skills must be updated continuously. Gone are the days when a programmer or systems analyst could say that his or her training was 'complete'. New automated analysis, design and programming tools are now dramatically accelerating software development. They will not make the programmer or analyst redundant—unless the programmer or analyst fails to get to grips with them.

The waves of innovation must be ridden, not ordered to turn back. When voice data entry sweeps through the offices of the world in a few years' time, the complaints of those who insist that their *only* skill is operating a keyboard will fall on deaf ears. Even the computers will be too busy, listening to the data.

Useful Addresses

ACE Centre (Aids in Communication in Education)
Ormerod School
Waynflete Road
Headington
Oxford OX3 8DD
0865 63508
Advises on suitable aids for learning, runs workshops, publishes booklets

AUCBE (Advisory Unit for Computer-Based Education)
19 St. Alban's Road
Hatfield
Hertfordshire
AL10 0HU

Acorn Computers Limited
Cambridge Technopark
645 Newmarket Road
Cambridge
CB5 8PD
0223 214411
Manufacturer of the BBC microcomputers

Amstrad
P.O. Box 462
Brentwood
Essex
CM14 4EE
0277 228888
Manufacturer of low-cost micros and word processing systems (also own the rights to the Sinclair microcomputers)

Apple Computer UK
FREEPOST
Information Centre
Eastman Way
Hemel Hempstead
Hertfordshire HP2 4BR
Manufacturer of the remarkable Macintosh microcomputer (and the earlier, worldwide best-selling, Apple II)

BARD/BARDSOFT
Handicapped Persons Research Unit
Newcastle-upon-Tyne Polytechnic
Coach Lane Campus
Newcastle-upon-Tyne
NE7 7TW
0632 326002
Data bases on research into aids for the disabled, and software available for special needs (which will run on popular computers)

BBC Publications (Schools)
P.O. Box 234
London
SE1 3TH

BCS (British Computer Society)
13 Mansfield Street
London
W1M 0BP
01-637 0471
Runs many specialist groups, including one for the disabled

BESA British Educational Software Association
4 Little Essex Street
London
WC2R 3LF
01-836 6633
Group of software publishers including some of the better ones; will supply catalogues

British LOGO User Group (BLUG)
Shell Centre for Mathematics
School of Education
University of Nottingham
Nottingham
Exchanges ideas via newsletters, conferences etc. Publishes *LOGOS*: a quarterly journal

CEDAR (Computers in Education as a Resource)
Imperial College Computer Centre
Exhibition Road
London
SW7
Research into computer-based and -assisted learning

CET (Council for Educational Technology)
3 Devonshire Street
London
W1N 2BA
Advisory body on many aspects of computers in education; publishes several useful pamphlets and information sheets

COIC (Careers and Occupational Information Centre)
MSC
Moorfoot
Sheffield
S1 4PQ
0742 704563
Publish range of materials including software simulations of e.g. running a hotel, supermarket, etc.

COMET (Concerned Micros in Education and Training), run by:
National Bureau for Handicapped Students
336 Brixton Road
London
SW9 7AA
01-737 7167
Make grants to young people who need microcomputers to assist their studies, but cannot raise the cash

Chiltern LOGO Project
AUCBE
Endymion Road
Hatfield
Hertfordshire
AL10 8AU
Originally under the aegis of the MEP (Microelectronics Education Project), concerned with LOGO use in primary education

Commotion
241 Green Street
Enfield
EN3 7SJ
Supply components for control applications (ask for catalogue)

Computer Education Group
North Staffs Polytechnic
Computer Centre
Blackheath Lane
Stafford

Data Protection Registrar
Springfield House
Water Lane
Wilmslow
Cheshire
SK9 5AX
0625 535777

Department of Education and Science
Publications Department
Honeypot Lane
Stanmore
Middlesex
HA7 1AZ

Department of Trade and Industry
Information Technology Division
29 Bressenden Place
London
SW1E 5DT
01-215 7877

Edinburgh LOGO Project
Department of Artificial Intelligence
University of Edinburgh
Forrest Hill
Edinburgh EH1 2QGL
Scotland
The major research on the use of LOGO in the U.K. was carried out here

GAPE (Geographical Association Package Exchange)
Department of Geography
Loughborough University
LE11 3TN

Gifted Children's Information Centre
941 Warwick Road
Solihull
West Midlands
B91 3EX

Information Technology Centres (ITeCs)
Department of Industry
Ashdown House
Victoria Street
London
SW1
01-212 3388
Funded by the DoI, ITeCs train young people in IT skills and help them to find employment

Institute for Educational Technology
The Open University
Walton Hall
Milton Keynes
Buckinghamshire
MK7 6AA
The OU have pioneered computer use in education; they also run a number of general computing courses

Lego U.K. Ltd.
Education Department
Wrexham
Clwyd
LL13 7TQ
Manufacture control packages including gears, pulleys, optical sensors, etc., interface with BBC micros

London and East Anglia Group
Miss Thompson, Correspondent of LEAG
'The Lindens'
Lexden Road
Colchester CO3 3RL
0206 549595
Comprises these examining boards: University of London, East Anglian, London Regional

MESU (Microelectronics Education Support Unit)
Science Park
University of Warwick
Successor to the MEP (Microelectronics Education Programme); a government-funded unit

MICE (Microcomputers in Computer Education)
Room 231C
The County Hall
London
SE1
Micros as applied in teaching computing topics

MUSE (Microcomputer Users in Secondary Education)
P.O. Box 43
Houghton-on-the-Hill
Leicestershire
A 'user' group, mainly teachers

Mathematics Education Centre
Upper Bognor Road
Bognor
Sussex

Midland Examing Group
Mr J L Reddaway, secretary to MEG
Cambridge University Local
Examinations Syndicate
1 Hills Road
Cambridge CB1 2EU
0223 61111
Comprises these examining boards: University of Cambridge, Oxford and Cambridge, Southern Universities, E. Midlands, W. Midlands

NATE (National Association for the Teaching of English)
49 Broomgrove Road
Sheffield S10 2NA

NESTEC
Keilder House
Newcastle-upon-Tyne Polytechnic
Coach Lane Campus
Newcastle-upon-Tyne
Components for buggies, robots, etc.

Northern Examining Association
Joint Secretary NEA
Joint Matriculation Board
Manchester M15 6EU
061-273 2565
Comprises these examining boards: Joint Matriculation, Assoc. Lancs. Schools, North, North West, Yorkshire and Humberside

North West Regional Examinations Board
Orbit House, Albert Street
Eccles M30 0WL
This board manages certain aspects of studies for areas covered by the Northern Association

Outset ITeC
18 Creekside
Deptford
London SE8
01-692 7141
An ITeC dedicated to training disabled young people in IT skills (ITeCs in other areas can also help, see ITeCs entry above)

RS Components Ltd.
P.O. Box 427
13 Epworth Street
London
EC2P 2HA

Research Machines Limited
Mill Street
Oxford
OX2 0BW
0865 248489
Manufacturer of the Nimbus (and the earlier RML 380/480 machines)

SEMERCs (Special Education Microelectronics Resource Centres)
Bristol SEMERC
Faculty of Education
Bristol Polytechnic
Redland Hill
Bristol
BS6 6U2
0272 733141

Newcastle SEMERC
Newcastle Polytechnic
Coach Lane Campus
Newcastle-upon-Tyne
NE7 7XA
0632 665057

Manchester SEMERC
Manchester College of Higher Education
Hathersage Road
Manchester
M13 0JA
061-225 9054

Redbridge SEMERC
Dane Centre
Melbourne Road
Ilford
Essex
IG1 4HT
01-478 6363
The SEMERCS train teachers, demonstrate hardware and software to ensure its effective use in teaching children with special needs

SEND: Special Educational Needs Database
Scottish Council for Educational Technology
74 Victoria Crescent Road
Glasgow
G12 9JN
041-357 0340

SMDP (Scottish Microelectronics Development Programme)
74 Victoria Crescent Road
Glasgow
G12 9JN

Secondary Examinations Council
Ms Sue Rhodes, Information Officer
Newcombe House
Notting Hill Gate
London
W11 3JB
01-229 1234
Monitors the GCSE syllabi and examinations to ensure that they meet the national criteria

Southern Examining Group
Mr P Burke, Organising Secretary SEG
Southern Regional Examinations Board
33 Carlton Crescent
Southampton SO9 4YL
0703 32312
Comprises these examining boards: Oxford, Associated, Southern, South East, South Western

TVEI (Technical and Vocational Educational Initiative)
Manpower Services Commission
Selkirk House
High Holborn
London WC1
01-836 1213

Technomatic Ltd.
17 Burnley Road
London
NW10 1ED
01-452 1500
Components

The Science Museum
Exhibition Road
London SW7
01-589 3456
Excellent computing exhibits

Watford Electronics
35 Cardiff Road
Watford
Hertfordshire
0923 40588
Components

Welsh Joint Education Committee
Mr G Lloyd Jones, Secretary
245 Western Avenue
Cardiff CF5 2YX
0222 561231

The following addresses are especially concerned with on-line applications:

Communitel
189 Freston Road
London W10 6TH
01-960 7998
Package enabling small viewdata services to be created

Distel (Display Electronics)
Free on-line catalogue of electronic components (transmits at 300 bps)
01-679 1888

Maptel (Maplin Electronics)
Catalogue available in large newsagents or on-line (300 bps)
0702 552941

Micronet 800
8 Herbal Hill
London EC1 5EJ
01-837 3699
A Prestel host enabling low-cost entry to telecommunications and electronic mail; caters for most popular microcomputers

One-to-One
Scorpio House
102 Sydney Street
London SW3 6NL
01-351 2468
Public electronic mail service

Prestel (BT's UK viewdata service)
Freephone Prestel
Very slow growth of subscribers was boosted by microcomputer users, gaining access through hosts, especially Micronet 800

Rewtel (Radio and Electronics World)
0272 236628
On-line catalogue of electronic components, transmits at 300 bps

TTNS (The Times Network Systems)
News International
Virginia Street
Wapping
London
E1 9DD
01-481 4100
Extensive local and national data bases, electronic mail, diary and bulletin board facilities available to schools and colleges

Telecom Gold
60-68 St Thomas Street
London
E1 3QU
01-403 6777
Public electronic mail service

The educational software illustrated in Chapter 18 is available from:

Mary Rose: Ginn & Co. Ltd.
Prebendal House
Parson's Fee
Aylesbury
Bucks HP20 2 QZ

Supergraph: Glentop Press Ltd.
Standfast House
Bath Place
High St
Barnet EN5 1ED

Iankey: Iansyst Ltd
Omnibus Building
41 North Road
London N7 9DP

Useful Reading

'T' and 'S' indicate reading suitable for teachers and students respectively

Directory of Opportunities in New Technology
Kogan Page (1985)
Useful mainly for older/qualified students; lists companies which may sponsor students through higher education
T

Educational Software Directory
Rickitt Educational Media
04065 5152
T

Acorn User
(magazine pub. by Redwood Publishing, 141–3 Drury Lane, London WC2B 5TF; available at larger newsagents)
At the time of writing, the leading magazine specifically aimed at BBC users
TS

BYTE
(magazine pub. by McGraw-Hill, available at larger newsagents)
Consistently good coverage of a wide range of computing topics: sometimes quite technical, rarely dull
TS

Computer Weekly
(magazine, pub. by Business Press International Ltd., controlled circulation)
One of the two leading industry weeklies: both business oriented, good news coverage, interviews, solid technical articles
TS

Computing
(magazine, pub. by VNU Business Publications, controlled circulation)
One of the two leading industry weeklies: both business oriented, good news coverage, interviews, solid technical articles
TS

Educational Computing
(magazine, unlikely to find it at newsagents, pub. Educational Computing Ltd., 8 Herbal Hill, London EC1R 5JB)
Good coverage across disciplines, useful software reviews
T

Working with Computers—A Guide to Jobs and Careers
National Computing Centre
Fair survey, but does not reflect recent developments: in particular the opportunities created by widespread use of micros
TS

Abelson, H. and di Sessa, A.
Turtle Geometry: the Computer as a Medium for Exploring Mathematics
MIT Press (1981)
Some good project ideas and notes on 'Turtle Procedure Notation': a machine-independent dialect of LOGO
T

Chandler, Daniel (ed.)
Exploring English with Microcomputers
National Association for the Teaching of English (UK), CET (1983)
T

Clarke, Arthur C.
2001: A Space Odyssey
New American Library, New York (1968) (& the Kubrick film) HAL, the super-intelligent computer with little respect for the human intellect, is a good starting point for discussion
TS

Daniels, A. and Yeates, D.
Basic Systems Analysis
Pitman
Good text for teachers interested in a more detailed treatment of systems analysis
T

Dawkins, C.
The Econet Micro Guide
Longman (1985)
A fairly technical guide to Acorn's own network
T

Day, N. & Rees, O.
Computer Spreadsheets
BBC Publications
TS

Duck, M.
Beginner's Guide to Microcomputer Languages
Newnes Technical Books (1984)
T

Equal Opportunities Commission
Girls and Information Technology
(available free from Publicity Section, EOC, Overseas House, Quay Street, Manchester M3 3HN)
Report on research on attitudes of younger pupils to IT, with particular reference to girls' and boys' expectations
T

Equal Opportunities Commission
Information Technology in Schools
(Guidelines for Good Practice)
EOC (1983)
T

Evans, Christopher
The Mighty Micro
The Impact of the Computer Revolution
Gollancz (1979)
In our view, a superb and prophetic book. Dr Evans' chronology of future developments is, however, a little optimistic.
TS

Freeman, R.
Structured BASIC
BBC/NEC (1984)
TS

Gascoigne, S.
Microchild Learning through LOGO
Macmillan (1984)
T

Goldenberg, P.
Special Technology for Special Children
University Park Press, Baltimore (1979)
Use of Turtle Graphics, etc. in special education
T

Green, F. *et al.*
Microcomputers in Special Education
Longmans/Schools Council (1982)
T

Hammond, R.
Computers and Your Child
Century Publishing Co. Ltd. (1984)
Valuable for parents and teachers
T

Hammond, R.
The On-Line Handbook
Fontana (1984)
Clear introduction to telecommunications, on-line data bases, viewdata, etc. Get an up-to-date edition!
TS

Hogg, R.
Microcomputers and Special Educational Needs: A Guide to Good Practice
National Council for Special Education (1984)
T

Howe, J.
Learning through Model-building, in Expert Systems in the Microelectronics Age
Michie, D. (ed.)
Edinburgh University Press (1979)
LOGO seen as a computerised construction kit
T

Jennings, M. and Smits, R.
Women's Computer Course Teaching Pack
National Extension College (1986)
T

Kelman, P. *et al.*
Computers in Teaching Maths
Addison Wesley (1983)
T

Marland, M. (ed.)
Information Skills in the Secondary Curriculum
Schools Council Curriculum Bulletin No. 9
Methuen (1981)
T

Michie, D. and Johnston, R.
The Creative Computer
Machine Intelligence and Human Knowledge
Viking (1984)
The leading UK exponent of artificial intelligence discusses how computers can, and will, create new knowledge
T

Napier, R. G.
Networking with the BBC Microcomputer
Prentice Hall (1984)
A good beginner's guide
TS

Noss, R.
Starting LOGO
AUCBE (1983)—see address list
T

Papert, Seymour
Mindstorms: children, computers and powerful ideas
Harvester Press (1980)
The definitive book on learning and LOGO. Cannot recommend too highly for *any* teacher
T

Peltu, M.
The Electronic Office
BBC Publications (1984)
Clearly written guide
T

Ross, P.
LOGO programming
Addison-Wesley (1983)
Thorough treatment and some good project ideas
T

Self, John
Microcomputers in Education: A Critical Appraisal of Educational Software
Harvester Press (1985)
Excellent, if slightly depressing, survey
T

Stonier, Tom
The Wealth of Information
Thames/Methuen (1983)
A powerful book: optimistic view of the future impact of information technology
T

Tagg, W. (ed.)
Parents' Guide to Educational Software
Daily Telegraph (1985)
Lists recommended software (get the latest edition), includes a guide to selection and several useful articles.
T

Turing, Alan M.
'Computing Machinery and Intelligence' in *Mind*
(1950), Vol. 59, pp 433–460
A classic paper for those interested in artificial intelligence: no use whatsoever for GCSE!
T

Weizenbaum, Joseph
Computer Power and Human Reason: From Judgement to Calculation
W. H. Freeman, San Francisco (1976)
The most cogently argued case against further development of artificial intelligence
T

Zorkoczy, P.
Information Technology: An Introduction
Pitman (1982)
T